Norbert Wolf

CASPAR DAVID FRIEDRICH

1774–1840

The Painter of Stillness

TASCHEN

HONG KONG KÖLN LONDON LOS ANGELES MADRID PARIS TOKYO

To stay informed about upcoming TASCHEN titles,
please request our magazine at www.taschen.com/magazine
or write to TASCHEN America, 6671 Sunset Boulevard,
Suite 1508, USA–Los Angeles, CA 90028,
contact-us@taschen.com, Fax: +1-323-463 4442.
We will be happy to send you a free copy of our magazine
which is filled with information about all of our books.

© 2007 TASCHEN GmbH
Hohenzollernring 53, D–50672 Köln
www.taschen.com

Project management: Juliane Steinbrecher, Cologne
Editing and layout: stilistico, Cologne
Translation: Karen Williams, Whitley Chapel
Cover design: Catinka Keul, Angelika Taschen, Cologne
Production: Martina Ciborowius, Cologne

Printed in Germany
ISBN 978–3–8228–1958–6

Contents

6
"The mystic with the brush"

16
"Art is infinite"

30
Nature as allegory

46
A journey to where?

68
"Dusk was his element"

94
Chronology

"The mystic with the brush"

In 1817 the Swedish poet Per Daniel Amadeus Atterbom visited the German painter Caspar David Friedrich in Dresden. A good thirty years later, he wrote down his recollections of the artist. With painstaking slowness, this strange character had placed his strokes one by one on the canvas, evoking for Atterbom the image of a "mystic with a brush". Mystical figures and brilliant geniuses were the heroes beloved of Romanticism. Youths wearing enthusiastic expressions or with dreamy eyes, artists who died young in the melancholy awareness of their social isolation peopled the portrait galleries of the years around 1800: the English poet Lord Byron, the German writer Novalis, the musical wunderkind Mendelssohn and the young painters Géricault in France and Runge in Germany. A picture in a similar vein exists of Friedrich, too: between 1806 and 1809, Gerhard von Kügelgen (1772–1820) painted the demonized portrait of his friend, seen in half-length and with the passion of Goethe's "Werther" in his gaze. Louise Seidler, the rather schoolmarmish painter who enjoyed Goethe's patronage and who from 1823 onwards was employed in the Weimar ducal household as drawing mistress to the princesses, was prompted by Friedrich's blue eyes and blonde sideburns to compare him to an ancient Teuton – admittedly, as she said, "a pious, femininely delicate one".

Another of his Dresden friends, Georg Friedrich Kersting (1785–1847), painted several portraits of Friedrich in his studio in the Dresden suburb of Pirnai, near the Elbe. In the version today in Berlin, the figure standing in front of his easel is no genius of the Storm-and-Stress era, but a domesticated husband (ill. p. 6). Palettes, a T-square and a rule are all that hang on the blank walls. On the bare floorboards, a spittoon. Friedrich, his visitors noted, had banished from his room any superfluous item that might disturb his concentration. One window is shut, the other has its lower half blocked by shutters and only its top half open to the grey-blue sky.

The painter who sees no world within himself should give up painting, insisted Friedrich. Only a brief extract is seen of the outside world; for everything else, the artist draws upon his imagination, which needs no constant external stimulus. Presented with this portrait, we can sense why later writers emphasized Friedrich's unsociable nature and his gruff exterior, defences which could be penetrated only with difficulty but which, once lowered, revealed a man of disarming amiability.

Gerhard von Kügelgen
The Artist Caspar David Friedrich, 1806–1809
Oil on canvas, 53.5 x 41.5 cm
Hamburg, Hamburger Kunsthalle

Georg Friedrich Kersting
Caspar David Friedrich in his studio, 1819
Oil on canvas, 51 x 40 cm
Berlin, Nationalgalerie, Staatliche Museen
zu Berlin – Preussischer Kulturbesitz

Friedrich's studio, spartan in its simplicity, has the nature of a meditation room, facilitating the artist's immersion in the world of his imagination.

*View from the Artist's Studio
(Right-hand Window),* 1805/06
Sepia over pencil, 31.2 x 23.7 cm
Vienna, Österreichische Galerie Belvedere

Portrait of a Man, c. 1808–1810
Oil on canvas, 51.7 x 42.4 cm
Hanover, Niedersächsisches Landesmuseum

If this is indeed a portrait of the artist's father,
Adolf Gottlieb Friedrich, it was probably
completed shortly before the latter's death
on 6 November 1809. Some suspect, however,
that it was painted from memory.

Around 1805 Friedrich made drawings of the two windows in his studio.
Particularly instructive is the view of the right-hand one (ill. p. 8). The interior
is reproduced in strict geometry and with the most economical of means. Standing in the shoes of the artist, whose face can be glimpsed in the mirror cut off by
the left-hand edge of the drawing, the viewer looks out through the open windows. From the bare confines of the studio, our gaze falls onto the landscape
that Friedrich – thus the message of his face, banished to the mirror – has inter-
nalized and transformed into a mental picture.

Just as Nature became a key concept in the philosophy of German Romanticism, so landscape assumes a central role in Friedrich's œuvre. Although figures,
including some that conceal identifiable individuals, are encountered throughout his work, he appears to have produced no more actual portraits after 1810.
One of the last of these – if it can in fact be attributed to Friedrich at all – is the
Portrait of a Man in Hanover, which may depict his father. The sort of landscape
in which Friedrich was chiefly interested, however, was never a simple imitation
of nature, but the result of a complicated interplay of visual impression and

mental and emotional reflection. Even an apparently topographical view such as the *Bohemian Landscape* in Stuttgart, which can be dated to c. 1810/11, represents a composite landscape made up out of several sketches. Zones of colour rise in layers up to the silhouetted mountain and the delicate yellow sky, "blueing" towards the top. From the two trees in the front middle ground, the view leaps precipitously into the misty distance. Spatial depth, the viewer senses, is possibly identical with a removal in thought and even time, albeit one eluding closer definition. Although such landscapes present us with a "virtual" reality, they never seem artificial, but simply exaggerated in their characteristics (cf. also ill. p. 10 bottom).

Friedrich's pictures are invariably underpinned by a rigorous structure, precise symmetries, geometric constructions and the contrast of verticals and horizontals – as indicated by the protractor and T-square hanging on the wall in Kersting's studio picture. Friedrich was never concerned with naturalistic impressions, but rather with "moodscapes", with pictorial spaces that resonate in the psyche. In Friedrich's own words, a picture must be *seelenvoll* – literally "full of soul" – in its effect if it is to meet the requirement of a true work of art. A composition based closely upon life or constructed according to academic rules might be "exemplary", but will fail to truly stir the viewer.

The Norwegian artist Johan Christian Clausen Dahl (1788–1857), who moved to Dresden in 1818, expressed it differently: the majority of Friedrich's contemporaries saw in his landscapes constructed ideas lacking truth to nature. "Friedrich bound us to an abstract idea…" later complained the Biedermeier painter Adrian

Bohemian Landscape, c. 1810/11
Oil on canvas, 70 x 104.5 cm
Stuttgart, Staatsgalerie Stuttgart

The painting, whose dating remains the subject of controversy, was formerly in the collection of Count Franz Anton von Thun-Hohenstein, who also owned Friedrich's *Tetschen Altar* (ill. p. 16). The mountains are part of the Milleschauer range, which lies south of Teplice in Bohemia.

Ludwig Richter (1803–1884). "With each passing year Friedrich wades ever deeper into the thick fog of mysticism; nothing is too mysterious or strange for him; he broods and struggles to pitch the emotion as high as possible," ran one article in an issue of the Tübingen *Kunstblatt* of 1820. It continued: "'Yes' – say his blind followers – 'one's imagination is allowed great scope!' This says very little; set up a blank canvas, and one's imagination is allowed even greater scope." In an issue of the *Blätter für literarische Unterhaltung* of 1827, on the other hand, this same freedom of interpretation becomes something to celebrate: "The fact that, in front of the works of this artist, the viewer is obliged to use his own powers of composition in order to fill them out, lends them … a strange fascination."

Even today, art-historical thinking remains ambivalent when it comes to the difficult question of the message conveyed by Friedrich's pictures. Can they and should they be interpreted in symbolic or even religious terms? It is best, according to one camp, to contemplate and comprehend them without words, just as the painter himself wished the viewer to do. Any attempt to analyse their moods more closely is superfluous. For Friedrich has created examples of typically Romantic introversion and testaments to the most isolated subjectivity. Others, on the other hand, see Friedrich's pictorial worlds as works of transcen-

Willem van de Velde
Seascape, c. 1660
Oil on canvas, 43 x 50,5 cm
Hamburg, Hamburger Kunsthalle

PAGE 13:
View of a Harbour, 1815/16
Oil on canvas, 90 x 71 cm
Berlin, Schloss Charlottenburg, Stiftung Preussische Schlösser und Gärten Berlin-Brandenburg

PAGE 14:
Woman at the Window, 1822
Oil on canvas, 44 x 37 cm
Berlin, Nationalgalerie, Staatliche Museen
zu Berlin – Preussischer Kulturbesitz

Window pictures are characteristic of German Romanticism. The tension between the sweep of the landscape outside and the intimacy of the interior corresponds in exemplary fashion to Novalis' demand that the poet should "romanticize" the world by lending the finite the guise of infinity.

Claude-Joseph Vernet
Seaport at Full Moon, 1771
Oil on canvas, 98 x 164 cm
Paris, Musée du Louvre

A number of Friedrich's views of ships and harbours orient themselves towards Vernet's paintings, which were known throughout Europe in the form of engravings.

dent, Protestant symbolism. Others again propose a middle way and insist upon taking greater account of Friedrich's recognizable links with tradition.

Playing a prominent role in Friedrich's œuvre are the themes of the sea, harbours and ships. Such motifs seem to have touched him deeply. This has led many writers to trot out various psychological and religious interpretations, often without pause for reflection. Let us examine, for example, the *View of a Harbour* of 1815/16, which may have been inspired by the harbour at Greifswald (ill. p. 13). It is evening, and between the masts of the two large ships in the middle ground stands the crescent of the waxing moon. Beneath it lie thin zones of colour, ranging from light yellow, orange and flaming red to lilac and grey on the horizon; above it, diagonal ribbons of cloud structure the sky. Within the almost unreal space thus created out of colour, the boats themselves are "floating" and seem to be moving forward out of the depths. The two large sailing ships are seen by some as symbolic motifs of departure and arrival. The harbour is thereby the final destination, the last resting-place, while the sky, and in particular the waxing moon, is a Christian symbol of hope. A comparison with Dutch marine painting of the 17th century, however, suggests that such interpretations should be treated with caution. The *Seascape* by Willem van de Velde (1633–1707), for example, operates with a similar repertoire. With its central visual corridor, rowing boat and low-lying horizon, it deploys the standard components of a "calm sea", a subject beloved since the Baroque and with no eschatological overtones. Friedrich has simply suppressed the details and tautened the composition in the verticals.

Some have also wanted to see an allegory of the end of life and a glorification of the Christian hereafter in *Evening on the Baltic Sea* (ill. p. 11), which arose towards 1831: the boats dragged up onto the shore, beside which two men are warming themselves at a fire, supposedly recall coffins. Friedrich, however, is here drawing upon an earlier composition of which any such interpretation would be incorrect, namely the painting *Seaport at Full Moon* by Claude-Joseph Vernet (1714–1789), executed in 1771 and reproduced and widely distributed in the form of engravings. But while the main motifs of *Evening on the Baltic Sea* reveal obvious parallels with those in Vernet's picture, in Friedrich's hands they evoke an atmosphere of greater stillness, which finds its formal equivalent in a more balanced grouping.

The scepticism that is directed against mystification should not, on the other hand, lead to the robbing of Friedrich's pictures of all deeper meaning. In the context of Romantic landscapes of emotion, of the Romantic outreach into the universal sphere and of the link, commonly made in Germany at that time, between utopian and religious aims, his pictures possess a fascinating dimension of depth. Thus while it is true that the painting *The Stages of Life* (ill. p. 90/91), executed around 1835, processes earlier traditions in its motifs, it also offers something more and new – namely the various stages of life between birth and death, and the ship as a symbol of life in the "sea" of the world. In interpreting the content of Friedrich's works, however, we should on no account forget his innovative formal language, as demonstrated in the *Seascape by Moonlight* from the period around 1830/35 (ill. p. 11). The ship's mast here provides the only vertical, placed in the centre of the composition in deliberate contrast to the horizontals of the sea, sky and the strips of light in the water, and in counterpoint to the diagonals of the clouds moving towards the right. However attractive the unearthing of hidden symbols may be, it is also important to recognize such compositional balance, which anticipates many of the principles of geometric and Construc-

tivist abstraction of the 20th century (cf. ill. p. 88). It is through precisely such structures that Friedrich distils vastness into singularity – as he is seen doing in this composition.

Which Friedrich is the "right" one – the one portrayed by Kügelgen or the one shown by Kersting? The brilliant visionary or the fastidious technician? In truth he was both. It is illuminating to compare Friedrich's *Self-portrait* (ill. p. 31), a chalk drawing of c. 1810, with the words of the Russian poet Vasily Andreyevich Zhukovsky, who met the artist in June 1821 and subsequently wrote back to St Petersburg: "Anyone who knows Friedrich's paintings of mist and … imagines him to be a contemplative melancholic with a pale face and poetic rapture in his eyes, is mistaken." Rapture is equally absent from Friedrich's own drawing of himself in around 1810. His eyes are piercing, a little sceptical. His figure, however, seems to be compressed into the lower half of the picture, as if the painter were looking up at the viewer, which is not the case. His right eye is positioned more or less in the centre of the composition. While the right-hand side of his face is brightly lit, the left lies entirely in shadow, whereby the eye here appears threatening. The face contains, as Jens Christian Jensen has pointed out, something schizoid.

Around 1810 Friedrich completed his first masterpieces, which brought him great public acclaim. According to a number of contemporaries, however, by this point in time he already had one suicide attempt behind him. This perhaps fell within the period 1801/02, during which he produced the drawings which his brother Christian would later (precisely when remains the subject of debate) execute in woodcut: *Woman with Spider's Web between Bare Trees* and *Woman (with Raven) beside the Abyss* – both undoubtedly images symbolic of transience. It would be wrong, however, to deduce from these that Friedrich's work is one of permanent hopelessness. "Death is the romanticizing principle of our life. Death is – life. Life is strengthened by death", writes Novalis. In the eyes of a Romantic, life on this side of the veil could even improve when viewed from this angle.

One of Friedrich's best-known paintings is his *Woman at the Window* of 1822 (ill. p. 14). Caroline Bommer, married to the artist since 1818, is the rear-view figure looking out through an open shutter onto the river Elbe below. Masts and rigging stand out against the section of sky. The viewer is once again struck by the calculated geometry of the composition; it is more expressive than the far-fetched attempt to interpret the subject in religious terms – the window cross as a Christian symbol, the far bank as the hereafter, and even the river as a symbol of death. The studio in which the woman is standing was one that Friedrich had rented since 1820. It reveals the same spartan simplicity as the earlier studio portrayed by Kersting (ill. p. 6). Here as there, nothing is to be allowed to distract the artist from his "mystic" work with the brush. As part of that work, *Woman at the Window* serves as a reflection of near and far, of a narrow interior and a spaciousness that can be sensed outside, of confinement within the here and now and a longing look beyond. Elements that recall the famous definition by Novalis: "By giving higher meaning to the mundane, a mysterious appearance to the normal, the distinction of the unknown to the known, the guise of infinity to the finite, I romanticize it." Romanticizing became Friedrich's passion and rapidly placed him at variance with the bourgeois spirit of the age. He nevertheless continued steadfastly down his own artistic path.

Woman with Spider's Web between Bare Trees,
1803/04
Woodcut, 16.8 x 11.8 cm
Hamburg, Hamburger Kunsthalle

The suggestion that Friedrich was drawing in this composition upon Dürer's engraving *Melancholia I* of 1514, as is often claimed, is improbable.

Woman (with Raven) beside the Abyss, 1803/04
Woodcut, 16.8 x 11.8 cm
Hamburg, Hamburger Kunsthalle

Like the previous illustration, this sheet also goes back to drawings from the year 1801, which the artist's brother Christian, a joiner, later issued as woodcuts.

"Art is infinite"

Caspar David Friedrich was born on 5 September 1774 in Greifswald. Friends spread the rumour that his family was descended on his father's side from a long-established line of counts, who were driven out of Silesia for their Protestant faith and had turned to the business of soap-making in Pomerania; others talked of a Swedish dynasty of counts. There is no documentary evidence either of such an aristocratic family tree or of any Swedish origins – although Friedrich's admiration for Sweden is something to which we shall be returning in another context (cf. pp. 27 ff.). Information regarding the family's financial circumstances is contradictory: thus it is recorded that the Friedrich household lived in poverty, yet elsewhere there is talk of a private tutor for the children, which would suggest a modest degree of prosperity. Friedrich's father was a strict Lutheran who passed on his excessively rigid moral principles to his children. The boy was confronted with death at an early age, when his mother died in 1781. The children were subsequently brought up by a housekeeper, "Mother Heiden", whom they treasured and loved. In 1787 one of Caspar David's five brothers, Johann Christoffer, drowned while trying to save him after he had fallen through the ice, and in 1791 his sister Maria died of typhus.

Once an important Hanseatic port, Greifswald had fallen to Sweden in the Thirty Years' War, together with the rest of West Pomerania (the region would only pass to Prussia in 1815). It had long since shrunk to just a provincial outpost on the Baltic and offered little to divert the young Friedrich's attention from the traumatic events of his childhood. Even the presence of the university failed to inject much life into the small medieval town. Around 1790, however, Caspar David took lessons from Johann Gottfried Quistorp, the drawing master at the university. Quistorp gave Friedrich a solid grounding – including in the field of architectural drawing – and awakened his love of nature and landscape. Quistorp's own extensive collection of paintings and drawings primarily comprised examples of Dutch and German art. Also at the university was the Swede Thomas Thorild, who was librarian and professor of literature and aesthetics from 1795 until his early death in 1808. Thorild taught that the physical (outer) eye was to be distinguished from what he classed as the superior spiritual (inner) eye – a distinction that would soon become highly important in Friedrich's thinking and painting, and whose origins lay less in German idealism than in English aesthetics.

View of Arkona with Rising Sun, c. 1803
Sepia, 65 x 98 cm
Hamburg, Hamburger Kunsthalle

The Cross in the Mountains
(The Tetschen Altar), 1807/08
Oil on canvas, 115 x 110,5 cm
Dresden, Gemäldegalerie Neue Meister,
Staatliche Kunstsammlungen Dresden

The painting's carved frame is based on a concept by Friedrich, but was executed by one of his friends, the sculptor Gottlieb Christian Kühn.

In 1794 Friedrich went to study at the highly-regarded Copenhagen Academy. He drew plaster casts of classical sculptures and studied Dutch landscape painting in the art galleries of the Danish metropolis. Teachers such as Nicolai Abildgaard (1743–1809), Christian August Lorentzen (1746–1828) and Jens Juel (1745–1802) represented an artistic trend positioned between classicism and a pre-Romantic emphasis upon feeling, and influenced by the "Norse" myths attributed to the bard Ossian (in actual fact, literary forgeries of the 18th century). The talented student was inspired both by this enthusiasm for the distant past and by Juel's carefully composed landscapes. Of the few drawings, watercolours and gouaches that survive from Friedrich's Copenhagen period, a number already reveal a sensitive eye for nature. *Landscape with Pavilion*, a watercolour drawing which arose around 1797, shows a motif from a landscape garden near Copenhagen (ill. p. 19). The nervous line and the pastel palette remain somewhat reminiscent of the Rococo. The subject testifies to the emotional emphasis which had always been associated in Europe with the English landscape garden and which, in the years 1779–1785, was explored in particular in Danish gardens by the garden architect C. C. L. Hirschfeld.

Friedrich left Denmark with many artistic stimuli. The years in Copenhagen had also introduced him to a spiritual world whose theology was strongly influenced by the mystical vision of nature expounded by the German poet Friedrich Gottlieb Klopstock (1724–1803). Not for nothing did the *Evangelium des Jahres*, published in Copenhagen in 1803, demand that the stations of the Church year be designated purely by landscape symbols. In 1798 Friedrich moved to Dresden, ducal residence and seat of government, famed for its magnificent art collections. The largely Protestant population was open to the ideas of the Enlightenment – at least until the armies of Napoleon marched in and occupied their city. Friedrich lived in a sparsely furnished house near the Elbe in Pirnai, a suburb settled by families who were not overly wealthy. If a visitor to Friedrich's studio wished to sit down, an old wooden chair would be fetched from another room; if two visitors came, a rickety bench had to be specially brought up.

Numerous drawings survive from Friedrich's early Dresden period, portraying landscapes, natural details and cityscapes. Friedrich's drawing style thereby matures from hesitant beginnings into confident outlines, fine hatching and a sophisticated handling of light and shade. While his early drawings demonstrate a preference for pen and ink and watercolour, from around 1800 he chiefly chooses to work in sepia. Brown sepia ink, used as a wash over a preliminary drawing, demands a subtle understanding of tonal values, and thus contemporary critics immediately recognized the masterly nature of Friedrich's drawings. In *View of Arkona with Rising Sun*, for example, a large sepia drawing of around 1803, it is almost incredible how Friedrich conjures an atmosphere of painterly solemnity out of the monochrome ink, which in places becomes almost red (ill. p. 17).

Precisely when Friedrich first experimented in oils remains the subject of dispute. Even if we attribute to him the *Wreck in the Sea of Ice* (ill. p. 20), dated 1798 and clearly Dutch-influenced, this must remain an isolated tentative attempt, since sepia drawings subsequently continue to dominate his output. Together with pen drawings, they also make up the majority of the landscape studies executed in 1801–1802 during a visit to Pomerania. It was on this trip that Friedrich saw, near Greifswald, the dilapidated Cistercian abbey of Eldena, whose ruins would run through his œuvre like a leitmotif (ill. p. 22).

Jens Juel
View across the Little Belt, c. 1800
Oil on canvas, 42.3 x 62.5 cm
Copenhagen, Thorvaldsens Museum

Friedrich was regularly represented in the Dresden art exhibitions of these years and his pictures were given a favourable reception in the art journals of the day. It was nonetheless surprising that they should also find acclaim in Weimar, the capital of German classicism – and furthermore in the art competitions which Johann Wolfgang von Goethe had instigated. Even though Heinrich Meyer, advisor to the prince of poets, was arch-conservative in his tastes, in 1805 Friedrich was awarded half the prize for two sepia landscapes. One was the *Pilgrimage at Sunset (Sunrise)* (ill. p. 22), a delicate landscape drawing infused with devotional intensity, which the judges in Weimar praised as being carefully executed and filled with a beautiful feel for nature.

"Elevation of the spirit" and "religious inspiration" were what Friedrich demanded of a true work of art. His opinion was shared by the members of his circle of friends in Greifswald, which formed in 1805 with the aim of founding a progressive Protestant church art. After all, King Gustav IV Adolf was about to introduce a new prayerbook and a constitution based on the Swedish model. The erudite pastor and poet Gotthard Kosegarten (1758–1818) would thereby play an important role. Outside the fishing village of Vitt near Cape Arkona, on the island of Rügen, he regularly delivered "shore sermons" in the open air. These soon became famous and subsequently appeared in print. In this atmospheric

Landscape with Pavilion, c. 1797
Pen, ink and watercolour, 16.7 x 21.7 cm
Hamburg, Hamburger Kunsthalle

As the atmospheric expression of a sentimental love of nature, the English landscape garden numbered amongst the sources of inspiration for many pre-Romantic and Romantic currents in Europe.

setting, the theologian testified to the divine revelation in nature. Since the weather was often bad, however, he also needed a chapel, plans for which were drawn up in 1805/06 by Friedrich himself. The artist thereby envisaged an elongated oval room with pews, and outside the entrance a similar oval in outline, in which rocks assumed the function of open-air seating. Napoleon's invasion of Germany in 1806 prevented work on the project from commencing; not until 1816, under the direction of an unknown architect, was the small octagonal chapel still standing today finally constructed. Both Friedrich and the second outstanding painter of German Romanticism, Philipp Otto Runge (1777–1810), were originally intended to paint altarpieces for the chapel, but only Runge's was ever completed: it depicts *St Peter on the Sea*, in which the true vehicle of religious expression is boundless nature, elevated even above the figures of the saints. The subject was especially apt in view of the fact that the congregation consisted chiefly of fishermen and seafarers, who – in Kosegarten's words – were to be reminded by the cross on the roof of "him who conjured up the storm and threatened the sea." Friedrich had met Runge, who had also been born in Pomerania and studied in Copenhagen, in Greifswald in 1801/02. After corresponding for many years on the subject of Romantic art and probably on Runge's important studies into colour, the two artists also met in person on a number of occasions. The fact that they were planning a joint trip to Rügen for the summer of 1806 – a trip which never actually took place – certainly suggests that they were relatively well acquainted. They cannot be said to have been close friends, however, as is sometimes claimed.

The events on Rügen can only have reinforced the Pietism practised in Friedrich's parental home and the mystical view of nature that went with it. August Wilhelm Schlegel (1767–1845) had already compared the solitary contemplation of nature with Communion, and Friedrich's friend Schwarz, the pastor who succeeded Kosegarten on Rügen, taught that the experiences gained in nature were the same as those obtained through the sacrament. Against such a backdrop, Friedrich believed in the spiritual capacities of art: "Thus man's absolute goal is not man, but the divine, the infinite. It is towards art, not the artist, that he should strive! Art is infinite, finite all artists' knowledge and ability." Since art, of course, cannot exist without the artist, this means that infinity can only be grasped in the finitude of artistic activity, issuing from the meditation cell of the studio.

Friedrich was now ready to explore this ideal in the medium of paint, too. 1807 saw him producing an increasing number of compositions in oil. *Summer*, which today hangs in Munich (ill. p. 23), unfolds in scenery unusually idyllic for Friedrich and takes as its theme the richness of life. The viewer's gaze falls in the foreground upon a pair of lovers in a bower, and from there meanders across a broad river valley to the gauzy silhouettes of the mountains providing the backdrop to this earthly paradise. The pendant to this painting, *Winter*, completed one year later, was destroyed when the Munich Glaspalast burned down in 1931; it depicted a sombre allegory of transience. *Mist* of 1807 (ill. p. 24/25) is housed in Vienna. Mist, which veils all objects, was considered in the 18th century either a metaphor for temptation and distance from God or for melancholy. Whether it may here be interpreted as a symbol of death seems questionable in view of the overall atmosphere, which seems to be brightening up. The Dresden *Dolmen in the Snow* (ill. p. 26) can also be dated fairly confidently to 1807. In 1828 Carl Schildener described the painting, which was then in his collection, as a "scene from the ancient fatherland" which depicted a dolmen near Gützkow, in the

Philipp Otto Runge
St Peter on the Sea, 1806/07
Oil on canvas, 116 x 157 cm
Hamburg, Hamburger Kunsthalle

Runge's painting was conceived as an altarpiece for a fishermen's chapel near Vitt on the island of Rügen, to which Friedrich was also to contribute a painting.

Wreck in the Sea of Ice, 1798
Oil on canvas, 29,6 x 21,9 cm
Hamburg, Hamburger Kunsthalle

The attribution of this painting to Friedrich is not undisputed. It is possible that the picture stems from the hand of a student friend in Copenhagen and that Friedrich gave it to relatives in Neubrandenburg, in whose possession it is later recorded.

vicinity of Neubrandenburg. The oak trees which so strikingly dominate the composition, and which stand within the lonely winter landscape like wounded giants, have been interpreted as symbols of a heathen past; it is more likely, however, that they visualize a patriotic pathos: "unbowed and defiant", as Schildener says, they outlive "the icy severity of foreign despotism".

Morning Mist in the Mountains (ill. p. 27), painted in 1808, is like a magnificent metaphor for the infinity of art claimed by Friedrich and thus for one of the prime objectives of German Romanticism. No more use of perspective to develop the pictorial space, no internal framework, no deployment of genre motifs for variety and no naturalistic local colour. In short, nothing more that an 18th-century connoisseur of academic art might admire. In their place we find masterly irritation: a bizarrely cleft mountain top in the morning mist, a scattering of spruce and Scots pine and a tiny cross on the summit, barely visible in the haze. As if he were floating, the viewer occupies no clear standpoint. What message is concealed behind this uniform scenery, and to what extent can references to Christian thought be identified? One answer lies in a comparison with another summit cross by Friedrich in *The Cross in the Mountains (The Tetschen Altar)* (ill. p. 16). The two-dimensional nature of this composition permits an only very limited sense of spatial depth. The few objects within the picture fuse into a clearly delineated elevation. The rocky pyramid rising upwards is no more than a silhouette, and seen against the light the foreground as a whole appears divested of material substance. Here, too, the viewer's standpoint remains undetermined. From the front edge of the painting, the steep slope leads straight up to the summit. Neither path nor staffage is to be found amongst the trees which gradually resolve themselves into shape into the shadowy foreground. Behind the triangle of the mountain, which starts from the left and right-hand corners of the picture, the sun lies low in the sky. It is not possible to tell from the painting whether it is rising or setting. It directs five geometricized rays of light upwards. Three of them disappear into the clouds; one produces a gleam on the crucified Christ, revealing the statue to be made of metal. The cross itself is located slightly to the right within the composition, its tip almost touching the apex of one of the gable-shaped banks of cloud behind. The base of the cross is wreathed in ivy,

Mist, 1807
Oil on canvas, 34.5 x 52 cm
Vienna, Österreichische Galerie Belvedere

The veiling of objects behind a curtain of mist
simultaneously lends their outlines a mysterious,
hieroglyphic intensity.

twining its way upwards the statue at the top. The statue's gaze is directed downwards and away from us, towards the sun whose sight is denied to the viewer. The painting is mounted in a gilt frame that was specially carved by a friend of Friedrich's, the sculptor Gottlieb Christian Kühn. At the bottom, a broad plinth is decorated with the eye of God and the symbol of the Trinity, flanked by vines and ears of corn. Rising to either side are what resemble multiple-rib pillars, surmounted by palm fronds which fuse into a pointed arch and are studded with five heads of angels. Above the middle head, in three-dimensional relief, is a silver star.

Over Christmas 1808 the painting, complete with frame, was put on display in Friedrich's studio with the windows shuttered, on a table covered with a black cloth, as if it were placed on an altar. It was seen during this period by Baron Friedrich Wilhelm Basilius von Ramdohr, who went on to write an article entitled "On a landscape painting intended as an altarpiece" for the *Zeitung für die elegante Welt* of 7 January 1809. It was a scathing review, criticizing the painting's lack of perspective and atmosphere and the placard-like stylization of its landscape elements. What Ramdohr condemned most strongly of all, however, was the tendency underlying the painting: through such works, landscape painting was trying to "steal into churches and creep onto altars". He considered the

Dolmen in the Snow, 1807
Oil on canvas, 61.5 x 80 cm
Dresden, Gemäldegalerie Neue Meister, Staatliche Kunstsammlungen Dresden

The dolmen portrayed here is probably one which stood near Gützkow, and which was removed between 1825 and 1829. Together with his drawing master Quistorp, Friedrich made several excursions to prehistoric burial sites.

Morning Mist in the Mountains, 1808
Oil on canvas, 71 x 104 cm
Rudolstadt, Staatliche Museen,
Schloss Heidecksburg

In 1808, a visitor to Friedrich's studio described
the painting he saw there as a mountain soaring
high into the clouds, on whose summit a cross
could be seen in the clear blue light. He was probably talking about the present painting, redis-
covered in 1941.

frame, which in his view symbolized the concept of Communion, to be tasteless.
Like many of Friedrich's Dresden acquaintances, as also a majority of modern
Friedrich scholars, Ramdohr thought the picture was destined right from the
start for the castle chapel at Tetschen (now Děčín) in Bohemia. The lord and
lady, Count Franz von Thun-Hohenstein and his wife, had already seen earlier
variations upon the same composition, such as the sepia drawing *Cross in the
Mountains* (ill. p. 29), and wanted – so the story went – to purchase the planned
final version. This last part is true. But it is also true that, at the beginning of
1808, the Countess reported with disappointment that Friedrich no longer
wanted to part with the painting which was now in progress because he wanted
to give it to his own sovereign. Since, as mentioned earlier, Friedrich's native
town of Greifswald was at that time Swedish territory, this sovereign was the
Swedish king Gustav IV Adolf, who had in fact paid several visits to Dresden
between 1803 and 1805. In 1981 Donat de Chapeaurouge showed that the iconographic elements of the *Tetschen Altar* can be understood as a reprise of the pictorial formulae with which, in the 17th century, Gustav II Adolf had proclaimed
his saving of Protestantism in Europe on printed leaflets and coins. This allegory
was transferred in the early 19th century to Gustav IV Adolf as the new saviour –
a process in which a decisive role was played Ernst Moritz Arndt (1769–1860),
the later poet of German liberation, who was himself a friend of Friedrich's and
who lived in the Swedish capital from 1806 to 1809. Gustav IV Adolf was one of
the earliest representatives of Romantic historicism on Europe's thrones and one
of the initiators of anti-Napoleonic countermeasures. And he won the affection

Detail of *The Cross in the Mountains*
(The Tetschen Altar), 1807/08 (page 16)

of German patriots when, after the dissolution of the Holy Roman Empire, he expressed the wish: "May I yet see the day when I behold Germany, as my second fatherland, restored to the standing to which its estimable nation and the fame of centuries give it an undeniable right."

In 1806 Napoleon had occupied most of the German states. Increasing bitterness stoked up hatred of the French and fed the awakening sense of German nationalism. Adrian Ludwig Richter vividly described the heated atmosphere in Dresden during this period in his book Lebenserinnerungen eines deutschen Malers (Memoirs of a German Painter): "It was not hard to prophesy war and military campaigns in those days; for since the start of the century, the dreaded man had shaken up everything in Europe, and Germany was groaning beneath his despotic fist. A poor, feverish shoe-mender … told some old women that the Revelation of St John talks specifically about this terrible war and even clearly names the French emperor who is bringing us all this suffering. In Hebrew he is called Abbadon, in Greek Apolion – and the French call him Napolion. He read it himself last night."

Johann Gottlieb Fichte gave his *Addresses to the German Nation* in the winter of 1807/08; in occupied Halle in 1807, Friedrich Daniel Schleiermacher, with whom Friedrich was in contact, combined the new Protestant movement with nationalism in his sermons and devoted himself energetically to religious reform. Arndt had meanwhile become a vocal patriot and in Prussia, Baron vom Stein, Hardenberg and Wilhelm von Humboldt had begun implementing some of their proposals for reform. In Dresden, which suffered particularly badly under French occupation, Friedrich's own thoughts – by no means confined to some strange inner world – radicalized into politically explosive engagement. The first reading of Heinrich von Kleist's *Die Hermannsschlacht* (Hermann's Battle) was probably held in his studio in 1808: a courageous undertaking in view of the clearly anti-Napoleonic stance of the play and omnipresent French censorship. During this period Friedrich also painted a picture, now lost, of an *Eagle above the Mist.* According to one contemporary, Friedrich gestured to the eagle with the words: "It will work its way out, the German spirit, out of the storm and the clouds," and emerge to find the "mountain tops which stand firm and have the sun." A cross surmounting such peaks – that was the future German national monument dreamed of by Arndt!

The *Tetschen Altar* was thus first and foremost not an altarpiece but a piece of political propaganda, a Cross in the Mountains which took up the liberation ideology of the Swedish monarchy: not without reason did Friedrich name his son, born in 1824, Gustav Adolf, and not without reason do ships flying the Swedish flag appear again and again in his seascapes (cf. ill. p. 88). The *Tetschen Altar* furthermore takes up Arndt's idea of the cross on the mountain top having the coded character of a national monument. In another article in the *Zeitung für die elegante Welt* of 17 January 1809, Baron von Ramdohr quotes Friedrich talking about the mountains which provided the material for the *Tetschen Altar* and which the artist visited at sunrise. If the sun in the painting was indeed originally rising, this would make it – in line with the cross – a symbol of hope. At the end of 1808, however, the situation changed dramatically. In Sweden, a military opposition formed against Gustav IV Adolf and the king was deposed. Although Friedrich was no longer able to present his *Cross in the Mountains* to his sovereign, he decided to finish the painting nevertheless and to sell it, complete with its new frame carved with religious symbols, to Schloss Tetschen. From this point on, it would appear from various newspaper articles, Friedrich described the sun in the picture as setting. He himself interpreted the painting as follows: "High up on the summit stands the cross, surrounded by evergreen fir trees, and evergreen ivy twines about the base of the cross. The glowing sun is sinking, and the Saviour on the cross shines in the crimson of the sunset … The cross stands on a rock, as unshakeably firm as our faith in Jesus Christ. Fir trees rise around the cross, evergreen and everlasting, like the hope of men in Him, the crucified Christ." When the artist wanted to visit Schloss Tetschen to see for himself how the painting had been displayed, the Count and Countess – both Catholics, incidentally – fobbed him off with excuses. For Friedrich's work was hanging not in the chapel but in the bedroom, next to an engraving of Raphael's *Sistine Madonna!*

The *Tetschen Altar* thus has a twofold history: having started out with a precise intention and a clear iconography, external circumstances forced a reversal in its polarity and obliged it to embrace concealment and obscuration. It is significant that the public in the Germany of the early 19th century were prepared, immediately and virtually completely, to abandon the first biography in favour of the second. A not inconsiderable proportion of modern scholarship has similarly accepted this second interpretation unchallenged, not least as a consequence of the popular cliché of the purely subjective introversion of German Romanticism.

Cross in the Mountains, c. 1805/06
Pencil and sepia, 64 x 93.1 cm
Berlin, Kupferstichkabinett, Staatliche Museen
zu Berlin – Preussischer Kulturbesitz

Nature as allegory

The Cross in the Mountains (The Tetschen Altar) brought Friedrich to the attention of a wider public. In these politically difficult times, scandal, sensation, admiration and support in print for Friedrich's work carried his name beyond the bounds of Dresden. Probably at no other point in his life did Friedrich enjoy more profound appreciation and greater admiration than in the years around 1810. Two landscapes in particular were responsible for thrusting Friedrich into the limelight. In 1810 they were exhibited as pendants at the Academy exhibition in Berlin, where they were purchased by the Prussian king Frederick William III. These two paintings also led directly to Friedrich's election – albeit by only a slender majority – as a member of the Berlin Academy. Both Goethe, who visited Friedrich in Dresden in September 1810, and the younger generation of Romantic poets recognized the two compositions as extraordinary works of art.

The first of the two is *The Monk by the Sea* (ill. p. 32/33), probably commenced in 1808 and undoubtedly a masterpiece in Friedrich's œuvre and the boldest picture within German Romanticism as a whole. Its composition breaks with all traditions. There is no longer any perspective depth whatsoever. At the bottom of the picture, the whitish sand dunes making up the narrow strip of shoreline rise at an obtuse angle towards the left. At their apex, the tiny figure of a man robed in black is visible from behind – the only vertical in the picture. There is no other staffage; even the two sailing boats which Friedrich had originally envisaged on either side of the man he subsequently painted over. The oppressively dark zone of the sea meets an extremely low horizon. Some five-sixths of the canvas is given over to the diffuse structure of the cloudy sky. The aim of this mode of representation, in which different, self-contained layers of the picture are arranged one behind or on top of the other, is to create an innovative, unlimited experience of space, something also evoked by the breath-taking effect of multiple coats of translucent glaze. It is more or less possible to maintain a sense of proportion as far as the horizon, particularly since the man provides something of a point of reference. The scale of the background, however, can no longer be grasped. Because all lines lead out of the picture, infinity becomes the true subject of the painting. In the awareness of his smallness, the man, in whose place the viewer is meant to imagine himself, reflects upon the power of the universe.

In an issue of the *Berliner Abendblätter* newspaper of 1810, Heinrich von Kleist, Clemens Brentano and Achim von Arnim published their now famous

Self-portrait, 1800
Black chalk, 42 x 27.6 cm
Copenhagen, Statens Museum for Kunst,
Department of Prints and Drawings

PAGE 30:
The Chasseur in the Woods, c. 1813/14
Oil on canvas, 65.7 x 46.7 cm. Private collection

PAGE 32/33:
The Monk by the Sea, 1808–1810
Oil on canvas, 110 x 171.5 cm
Berlin, Nationalgalerie, Staatliche Museen zu
Berlin – Preussischer Kulturbesitz

This composition is rightly considered the
boldest work of German Romantic painting.

Gustave Courbet
The Coast near Palavas, 1854
Oil on canvas, 39 x 46 cm
Montpellier, Musée Fabre

The avant-garde composition of Friedrich's
Monk by the Sea (ill. p. 32/33) drew a clear response later in the 19th century, for example in the work of Courbet and James Abbott McNeill Whistler.

Page 35 bottom:
The Abbey in the Oak Wood, 1808–1810
Oil on canvas, 110.4 x 171 cm
Berlin, Nationalgalerie, Staatliche Museen
zu Berlin – Preussischer Kulturbesitz

Friedrich took up this motif once again in his painting *Monastery Graveyard in Snow* of c. 1817–19, where he rendered it even more monumental. This important painting was destroyed in Berlin in 1945.

description of the painting, in which they speak of "apocalyptic featurelessness" and "boundlessness", and which culminates in the striking image that, since the picture has no foreground but its frame, it is "as if one's eyelids had been cut off". Kleist defines the enormous modernity of the painting, which removes the actual artistic creative process into an intermediary realm of the imagination: "What I wanted to find within the picture itself, I found only between myself and the picture." In braving such a step, Friedrich was able to refer in part to precedents in Dutch Baroque painting, such as the foreground of the *View of Delft* (c. 1660/61) by Jan Vermeer (1632–1675). There, however, the exposed nature of the figures on the empty shore in the foreground and the unbounded reach of the view to either side are cushioned by the main horizontal of the townscape, which lends them a formal and iconographic stability. In Friedrich's painting, on the other hand, the individual confronted by the desolate universe is homeless. Kleist identified the small figure of a man as a monk, and specifically as a Capuchin friar. Friedrich himself described the figure as a sort of Faustian thinker, musing in front of the inscrutable hereafter. Friedrich had probably actually read Goethe's *Faust*, which was published in 1808. Whatever the case, we should not dismiss the designation of "monk" too lightly, for the figure primarily represents an exemplary embodiment of tragic existentialism. The painter Carl Gustav Carus (1789–1869) later gave the picture the neutral title of *Wanderer on the Sea Shore*, and thereby named a motif which would continue to surface in painting over the following years, even if the great French realist Gustave Courbet (1819–1877), in *The Coast near Palavas* of 1854, for example, would combine the exposure of man with the pathos of the figure of the conscious seeker.

The pendant to *The Monk by the Sea* is *The Abbey in the Oak Wood* (ill. p. 35), dating from the same period. With its oaks and Gothic ruins – based on the ruins of Eldena monastery (ill. p. 22) – Friedrich is probably referring to the pre-Christian era of natural religion and to the Christian Middle Ages. The cortège of monks has proceeded past an open grave to arrive at the portal of the church, beneath which stands a crucifix flanked by two lights. In 1821 the Dresden painter Ernst Ferdinad Oehme (1797–1855) magnified this motif as if with a telephoto lens, although in his painting the cathedral towers into the sky as an intact stronghold (ill. p. 35). In Friedrich's picture, lastly, the possibility of a better world seems to reveal itself only on the pale horizon, on the far side of history and death. Carus, a fellow artist and a personal friend of Friedrich's since 1817, described the painting and its solemn symmetry as perhaps the "most profound poetic work of art of all recent landscape painting"; later he would turn his back on Friedrich and credit his work with a "morbid flavour". Dismissive voices, such as that of the Berlin classicist sculptor Gottfried Schadow (1764–1850), who ascribed the subject a "pedestrian tone", remained in the minority – and rightly so, according to modern thinking.

What comes to the fore in these two canvases is what would characterize Friedrich's manner of composition from now on and what would set him apart from the classical tradition: the elements of a "negative beauty" – deliberate monotony, formal repetition, the unmistakable sound of emptiness within the orchestral whole of the picture, and the strange coupling of proximity to nature and distance from nature. The individual motifs are permeable to emotional nuances and produce analogous sensations in the viewer. The same is true of the beautiful *Mountainous Landscape with Rainbow* of around 1810 (ill. p. 36). Its dreamlike atmosphere results not least from the two light sources at work within the composition: one behind the viewer, i.e. the sun, whose light produces the phenomenon of the rainbow and illuminates the foreground and the figure signifying Friedrich himself, and the other above the top of the arch, in this case the moon, which is breaking through the clouds. Day and night meet. Leaning against the rocks, which may symbolize the unshakeable nature of faith, the small figure of the man is looking up at the sublime natural spectacle and towards the gloomy mountains in the background, from which he is separated by a valley of unfathomable depth. Over the ghostly earth sinking into dark shadow, the rainbow arches as a biblical sign of the reconciliation between God and man. Wonderment, reverence and contemplation are the appropriate reactions to the elements of nature. Friedrich is offering us not a realistic portrayal of a geographical region with a walker, but an emblematic topography whose meaning can be traced back in part to the theosophical pictorial tradition of the 18th century and the writings of the mystic Jakob Böhme of the early 17th century.

Morning in the Riesengebirge (ill. p. 37) from the years 1810/11 may be seen as a sort of continuation of the *Tetschen Altar*. The subject goes back to sketches which Friedrich made during a walking tour of the Riesengebirge mountains, undertaken in July 1810 in the company of his friend Kersting, even if the overall view does not adhere slavishly to actual topographical reality. The large painting was exhibited in Berlin in 1812, before being purchased by the Prussian king. Reviews of the day compared the strictly two-layered composition and the undulating crests of the mountain ridges with Friedrich's seascapes. The brown rocks in the foreground culminate in a jagged pinnacle surmounted by a cross. This solid mass of rock is separated from the misty mountain ranges in the background by a bottomless chasm. The light strip of the expansive horizon announces the rising sun. The figure of a blonde, lightly-clad woman is drawing a man to her

Ernst Ferdinand Oehme
Cathedral in Winter, 1821
Oil on canvas, 127 x 100 cm
Dresden, Gemäldegalerie Neue Meister,
Staatliche Kunstsammlungen Dresden

and to the cross – these two tiny figures may have been painted into the picture by Kersting, at Friedrich's request. Older and more recent interpretations of the painting vary between the patriotic and the religious. The woman is usually taken to be an allegory of faith beneath the sign of the cross and in front of the salvation promised on the horizon. The man who is being led up to the highest point in this "landscape of salvation" is thought to be Friedrich himself.

In a philosophical treatise of 1757, Edmund Burke (1729–1797) prepared the way for an aesthetic of the sublime based on the categories of overwhelming grandiosity and subjective stimuli which lay bare the depths of the human psyche. These manifest themselves in particular in the realm of nature, in the rocky massifs of the high mountains, in chasms, where pure space unfolds downwards, and by the sea, where the horizon extends into boundless breadth. The notion of the sublime ran through all Romantic currents and found its ideal expression at Friedrich's hands, not simply owing to his choice of theme, but above all on account of his stylization of landscape, his renunciation of rational space and the comfortable idyll, and his emphasis upon the boundless. The sublime, Romanticism and Friedrich's œuvre also provided important stimuli for the Hudson River School which formed in America the 1820s, and whose landscape painting celebrated the solemn wilderness and enormous scale of the North American continent as a direct expression of divine creation. If we compare the *Cross in the Wilderness* of 1857 (ill. p. 37) by Frederick Edwin Church (1826–1900) with Friedrich's *Morning in the Riesengebirge* (ill. p. 37), such links become transparent. It is true that, whereas Friedrich's summit cross is a symbol

Mountainous Landscape with Rainbow, c. 1810
Oil on canvas, 70 x 102 cm
Essen, Museum Folkwang

It has been suggested that here, as in other of Friedrich's paintings, the small figures may have been executed by his friend Georg Friedrich Kersting. This remains hypothetical, however.

of a landscape redeemed by Christ, Church's landscape is set in Ecuador and strikes a resignedly melancholy tone in its juxtaposition of the wayside calvary and the rocky peak standing out darkly against the glowing sunset. In the drawing of the contours of the mountains, and in the sense of infinite breadth and the renunciation of all stabilizing framing elements, the two paintings clearly correspond.

If we remember the political message originally hidden in the nature symbolism of the 2, subsequently obscured to avoid censure by the French occupying forces, it is by no means unlikely that Friedrich should have attempted to convey something similar in some of his later landscapes. When, namely, Napoleon's Russian campaign collapsed in 1812 and the Wars of Liberation were launched against the French in 1813, Friedrich once again showed himself act-ively committed to the cause. It is true that he did not respond to the call to arms followed enthusiastically by his friends Kersting, the poets Theodor Körner (1791–1813) and Baron de la Motte Fouqué (author of the romance *Undine*, 1777–1843), and the painters Philipp Veit (1793–1877) and Ferdinand Olivier (1785–1841), who joined up as more or less short-term guerrillas; the not yet 40-year-old Friedrich considered himself too old. But he was happy to contribute financially towards equipping the volunteers. It was also during these years, between 1812 and 1814, that he executed his two clearly political paintings of the tomb of Arminius, both of which he first carefully explored in preparatory studies. In the Bremen version (ill. p. 38), Friedrich offers us a landscape of primeval forests and mountains. Our view falls through a funnel-shaped opening in the foreground onto a steep rockface, whose vertical wall extends the composition upward beyond the bounds of the frame. It gives way below to a view of a cave, in front of which the

Morning in the Riesengebirge, 1810/11
Oil on canvas, 108 x 170 cm
Berlin, Nationalgalerie, Staatliche Museen
zu Berlin – Preussischer Kulturbesitz

This picture, which was purchased by the King of Prussia, must have arisen shortly after Friedrich's return from his tour of the Riesengebirge mountains, undertaken with Kersting in July 1810. It is one of the largest paintings in his entire œuvre.

Frederick Edwin Church
Cross in the Wilderness, 1857
Oil on canvas, 41.3 x 61.6 cm
Madrid, Museo Thyssen-Bornemisza

Rocky Valley (The Tomb of Arminius), 1813/14
Oil on canvas, 49.5 x 70.5 cm
Bremen, Kunsthalle Bremen

Badly damaged in the Second World War, the missing
upper third of the painting has been replaced by a
hand-tinted photograph.

Tombs of the Fallen in the Fight for Independence
(Tombs of Ancient Heroes), 1812
Oil on canvas, 49.3 x 69.8 cm
Hamburg, Hamburger Kunsthalle

The letters GAF on the obelisk perhaps stand for the initials of someone
who fell in the Wars of Liberation. Such use of code was often necessary in
order to escape the censorship imposed by the French occupying forces.

lost-seeming figure of a French chasseur is gazing at a weathered sarcophagus. Its inscription, written in German and formerly legible, runs (translated): "May your loyalty and invincibility as a warrior forever be an example to us." The words are thought to refer to Arminius (also known as Hermann the Cheruscan), the Germanic chieftain who won a victory over the Romans in the early 1st century CE (possibly in the version of the story given in Kleist's *Hermannsschlacht*), or more generally to a soldier who had fallen in the Wars of Liberation. Coupled to the hope of freedom for the German people was ultimately also a desire for a great leader. The name of Arminius is also found on the demolished grave in the foreground of *Tombs of Ancient Heroes* (ill. p. 39), a comparable composition in which the rocky cave is seen enlarged in close-up. Further inscriptions within this composition clearly testify to the patriotic character of the painting and its reference to the wars against Napoleon.

Friedrich's perhaps best-known and certainly his clearest political work is *The Chasseur in the Woods* (ill. p. 30). It was commenced in summer 1813 and went on show in the Exhibition of Patriotic Art mounted in Dresden in March of the following year. It was accompanied by the information that the lost chasseur was listening to the sound of his own funeral dirge, being sung by the raven on the tree stump. A similar description is found in a catalogue note by Prince Malte von Putbus, the painting's first owner, himself amongst those who had distinguished themselves in the Wars of Liberation. It states: "It is a winter landscape; the rider, whose horse has already been lost, is hastening into the arms of death;

The Garden Terrace, c. 1811/12
Oil on canvas, 53.5 x 70 cm
Berlin, Schloss Charlottenburg, Stiftung Preussische Schlösser und Gärten Berlin-Brandenburg

Whether this view shows the park attached to the palace in Erdmannsdorf remains the subject of dispute. The details of the background landscape argue against such a conclusion.

a raven is crowing a funeral dirge after him." In oppressive solitude, the soldier has halted in a forest clearing. The tracks he has left in the snow will soon also disappear. Presented with the hopelessness of this situation, few of Friedrich's contemporaries could have failed to think of the collapse of the Napoleonic army under the grip of the Russian winter. It is also possible that the tall fir trees, standing in closed ranks, are intended to symbolize German patriots, and the young pines near the tree stumps in the foreground the post-war generation.

Not every landscape from these years can be ascribed a political dimension. This is certainly not the case in *The Garden Terrace*, a painting of haunting tranquillity that arose around 1811/12 (ill. p. 40). The powerful verticals of the two chestnut trees and the horizontal of the path running parallel to the lower edge of the canvas describe a rectangle in which a woman reading a book, a marble statue and the stone lions flanking the gate are assembled like the elements of a still life. The gate, which incorporates an ornamental cross and behind which a peaceful landscape extends away out of the picture, is the key motif: beyond its mighty lions lies the realm of distance and departure, while on this side lies the zone of contemplation – both spheres nevertheless married by an exquisite harmony and pictorial geometry.

Free from political content, too, is probably Friedrich's *Winter Landscape* of 1811 in Schwerin, which has its counterpart in a *Winter Landscape with Church*

Winter Landscape, 1811
Oil on canvas, 33 x 46 cm
Schwerin, Staatliches Museum

Winter Landscape with Church, 1811
Oil on canvas, 33 x 45 cm
Dortmund, Museum für Kunst und Kulturgeschichte der Stadt Dortmund

In a letter of 22 June 1811, written by Friederike Volkmann in Dresden to
the psychologist Dr Christian August Heinroth in Leipzig, this painting is
described as the pendant to the *Winter Landscape* (ill. p. 41) in Schwerin.

The Cross in the Mountains, 1812
Oil on canvas, 44.5 x 37.4 cm
Düsseldorf, museum kunst palast

in Dortmund (ill. p. 42). The Schwerin painting is characterized by the sombreness of an expanse of snow stretching away into the infinite distance, which modern interpreters see as a symbol of death, a nihilistic sign of doom. Contemporary critics were more reserved. In an article in the *Journal des Luxus und der Moden* of 1812, the painting is described thus: "A snowy expanse with few interruptions is divided in the simplest fashion into three grounds. The middle ground and foreground reveal a few bare tree trunks … between which stands a man stricken in years, leaning on crutches, who is probably intended as a play upon the winter of life and thus bears an allegorical relationship to the landscape." The pendant in Dortmund introduces, for the first time in Friedrich's œuvre, a Gothic church, seen as a monumental vision emerging out of the mist like a phantasmagoria and rising against the gloomy background of a winter sky. Nearer the viewer, a man is leaning back against a boulder and gazing up the crucifix in front of a cluster of young fir trees. He has flung his crutches demonstratively far away from him into the snow. This combination of motifs has been interpreted as a reference to the security of the Christian in his faith, and since a religious view of the world was closely associated with a patriotic stance in the ideology of the liberation movement, Friedrich's composition is correspondingly also thought to express a hope for political salvation.

Visions of Gothic architecture appear regularly in the artist's work from now on, rising like a man-made enigma in a mysterious landscape scenario. An instructive example is provided by *The Cross in the Mountains* (ill. p. 43), which can be dated fairly confidently to 1812, and which has long been viewed as a further development of the *Tetschen Altar*. The rough and rocky terrain of the foreground surrounds a spring, behind which, within an indeterminate space, rise a dark wall of fir trees and the gabled façade of a Gothic church, reduced to a shadowy silhouette. A wayside calvary marks the border between foreground and background. The logic of space and time seems to have been abandoned in this painting in favour of the unreality of a dream.

The seemingly unreal atmosphere of such pictures should not be taken to mean, however, that they are devoid in every case of more specific content. For it should not be forgotten that the revival of the Gothic style, as expressed in the vocabulary of the neo-Gothic, was understood as a call to forward-looking religious and political reform. Reflecting upon the medieval past, which was considered part of the national heritage, was intended to release the forces of all Germans to shape the nation of the future. The progressive impulse now conveyed by an enthusiasm for the Middle Ages manifested itself in particular in works by the neo-Classical Berlin architect Karl Friedrich Schinkel (1781–1841). Between 1810 and 1815 Schinkel was primarily active as a painter and was influenced both stylistically and in his choice of subject matter by Friedrich, conceiving Romantic medieval dreams of Gothic cathedrals. Like his plans for a monumental neo-Gothic cathedral as a monument to the fatherland, these went hand in hand with the bourgeois patriotism and liberal nationalism accompanying the Wars of Liberation in Germany. Within this heady environment, Friedrich devoted himself intensively to plans for monuments to fallen heroes of the Wars of Liberation (ill. p. 45). One of these designs proposes a stele, flags, coats of arms, martial figures and crossed swords. With a confident feel for architectural and decorative values, formal elements of the Empire style, with its Egyptian leanings, are combined with medieval symbols into a "Romantic classicism".

When an exhibition of patriotic art was organized in March 1814 under the patronage of the Russian governor-general Prince Repnin, commander of the

Wilhelm Ahlborn after Karl Friedrich Schinkel
Gothic Cathedral by the Water, 1823
Oil on canvas, 80 x 106.5 cm
Berlin, Nationalgalerie, Staatliche Museen
zu Berlin – Preussischer Kulturbesitz

In this reliable copy after a painting by Schinkel, (c. 1813/14) a monumental Gothic cathedral – created from the artist's imagination and understood as a symbol of national liberation – is seen against the light. The setting sun and the threatening storm clouds overhead imply a reference to impending war and departure.

Monument with Colourful Flags, um 1814/15
Black pen and Indian ink over pencil,
55.2 x 43.3 cm
Mannheim, Städtische Kunsthalle

In addition to monuments to fallen soldiers,
Friedrich continued to design tombs for private
individuals even into the 1820s. A number of
tombstones executed to his designs have been
identified in Dresden cemeteries.

tsarist troops who liberated Dresden from the French, Friedrich submitted *The Chasseur in the Woods* (ill. p. 30), *The Tomb of Arminius* (ill. p. 38) and *Tombs of Ancient Heroes* (ill. p. 39), as well as a sepia drawing. His artist colleague and friend Dahl later recalled that many people, "primarily during the period of the Wars of Liberation, sought and found" in Friedrich's pictures "a specific, I would like to say politically prophetic meaning, references to an almighty, invisible hand intervening in the confused affairs of men and in the liberation of Germany from the foreign yoke." The Romantics used the period of French occupation to draw attention to the German people, so long dismissed and downtrodden, to its songs, myths and sagas. With the discovery of "The Song of the Nibelungen," they restored to Germany its national epic. The redefinition of what it meant to be German provided the intellectual backdrop to the war of 1813. Scharnhorst's citizen army – in place of an army of mercenaries – was a military expression of a Romantic view of the State. But all hopes proved vain. In a letter to Arndt of 12 April 1814, Friedrich prophesied: "As long as we remain serfs to princes, nothing great… will ever happen. Where the people have no voice, they are also not allowed to have any sense of themselves as a people or to honour themselves."

A journey to where?

The Early Romantics – first the poets and philosophers, then the fine artists and musicians – started out with high ideals: external events, the struggle against Napoleon and the hopes of becoming a nation, together with the emancipation of the individual, were to bring about a new and better world. Social reality stood firmly in the way of such ambitions, however. As a consequence, a number of individuals became aware relatively quickly of the final character of Romanticism. Thus Gotthilf Heinrich Schubert, an acquaintance of Friedrich's, wrote as early as 1810: "The age treats us harshly! The young people, seemingly so full of promise and energy, who some six years ago wanted to storm the intellectual skies, the most industrious champions of the new school, who wanted to bring Germany a new golden age more brilliant than the first, a new blossoming of poetry and science – where have they gone?" Following the defeat of Napoleon, the Congress of Vienna of 1815 had ushered in an era of anti-liberal "restoration", masterminded by Metternich, in which Early Romanticism's political dreams of a proud German citizen came to an end. The authorities made ruthless use of their police machines, both official and secret, to silence outspoken individuals and to forestall any criticism in literature or art. According to contemporary accounts, Austria and Prussia, in their intolerance of their citizens, were second to none when it came to censorship and the persecution of "demagogues".

Caspar David Friedrich now began, little by little, to resign himself to the circumstances. The Friedrich who had carried poetry in landscape to an incomparable intensity and lent expression not just to subjective moods and feelings, but also to a non-denominational spiritual religiosity – and invested all of that in a political vision – took a step back. Nothing great could be achieved by "serfs to princes" and he had never wanted to be one of those, and hence virtually all that remained to him was to withdraw into his own private world. In 1821 he admitted to the Russian poet, Zhukovsky: "I must surrender myself to what surrounds me, unite myself with its clouds and rocks, in order to be what I am. I need solitude in order to communicate with nature." Even in his solitude, however, Friedrich never quite lost sight of his former ideal, to achieve something "great". This distinguishes him from many of his fellow-artists. From 1815 onwards, Friedrich increasingly turned to the motif of the coast and the harbour (ill. p. 13) – perhaps a first indication that, from now on, his imagination would be taking him inside, into the world of his personal yearnings, rather than steering him towards external "patriotic" themes.

Georg Friedrich Kersting
Caspar David Friedrich Walking in the Riesengebirge, 1810
Watercolour and pencil on paper, 31 x 24 cm
Berlin, Staatliche Museen zu Berlin – Preussischer Kulturbesitz, Department of Prints and Drawings

Neubrandenburg, c. 1817
Oil on canvas, 91 x 72 cm
Greifswald, Pommersches Landesmuseum

The anti-liberal policies of the new German Confederation took their toll. Arndt was dismissed from his teaching post. General Scharnhorst, who died of wounds sustained in battle in 1813, received no tribute on account of his liberal ideas. In Berlin, the theologian Friedrich Schleiermacher soon numbered amongst the "troublesome elements". Imprisonment awaited all those who became victims of the persecution of demagogues which followed the Karlsbad Decrees of 1819. Friedrich, who in 1816 had finally been made a member of the Dresden Academy with a salary of 150 thalers, thus had every reason to be wary, even in Saxony. After this date, the Prussian royal family never again purchased a single one of his works. It was during this period that Friedrich produced the painting *Neubrandenburg* (ill. p. 46). Soaring high above the town, which is seen in silhouette from the northeast, is the slender spire of the Marienkirche. The hilly landscape on the horizon, above which grandiose banks of clouds unfurl into an enormous sky, is the product of pure imagination. This has led some art historians to conclude that the work is not intended as a straightforward *vedutà*, but as a glorification of Gothic Neubrandenburg. The two men on the track in the foreground stand motionless beside what is probably a dolmen and contemplate the cityscape in the distance. Opinions differ as to whether the lighting conditions represent sunrise or sunset. Like the bushes shedding their leaves in the foreground, the migratory birds in the sky, probably storks, serve as pointers to approaching winter and thereby to death.

Picture in Remembrance of Johann Emanuel Bremer, c. 1817
Oil on canvas, 43.5 x 57 cm
Berlin, Nationalgalerie, Staatliche Museen zu Berlin – Preussischer Kulturbesitz

The painting is dedicated to Bremer, the physician and pharmacologist who died on 6 November 1816 at the age of seventy. Bremer's contribution to the advance of medicine in Berlin lay primarily in his work on the smallpox vaccination.

Generally dated to around 1817, Friedrich's *Picture in Remembrance of Johann Emanuel Bremer* is imbued with infinite and mysterious calm (ill. p. 48). In its layout, the oil painting recalls the earlier *Garden Terrace* of 1811/12 (ill. p. 40), except that the atmosphere now appears even more intense, more removed from reality, more solemnly sublime. Appearing within the central garden gate is the inscription "Bremer". The name refers to one of Friedrich's countrymen, a doctor practising in Berlin who introduced the smallpox vaccination into the city. Friedrich, who had a strong social conscience, knew and admired Bremer, who devoted himself to caring for the poor. The present painting arose following Bremer's death in Berlin on 6 November 1816. The bare foreground has been interpreted as symbolizing the poverty of earthly existence, albeit one lent Christian value by the vine as a symbol of the Eucharist. Like the poplars, the garden gate serves as a memorial and symbol of death, beyond which opens up the hereafter, bathed in the light. Although such an interpretation may sound far-fetched, it does not lie outside the bounds of possibility; in 1811, for example, following the death of Queen Luise, Frederick William III had ordered the wooden gates through which, on her final visit, his wife had left the park of Schloss Paretz, to be replaced with wrought-iron gates bearing her monogram. Whatever the case, Friedrich here succeeds in creating one of the most impressive atmospheric images of German Romanticism – one nocturnally subdued in mood. He also infuses the pictorial plane, moreover, with a harmonious geometric rhythm, as articulated in the symmetry of the overall composition and the visual leaps between the uprights of the pergola, the trunks of the poplars and the silhouetted church spires and ship's masts in the background.

On 25 January 1817, Stralsund council voted to invite Karl Friedrich Schinkel and Caspar David Friedrich to submit plans for a new neo-Gothic choir for the town's Marienkirche. Friedrich's designs, which were never executed, envisaged a unification and consolidation of the interior from the altar to the crossing piers with the aid of wood cladding. The training in architectural drawing which Friedrich had received from Quistorp once again stood him in good stead. But the artist was interested in more than just form alone. "In a building where people gather to humble themselves before God, before Him for whom rank is of no regard, surely all distinctions of class should cease; the rich man should feel here, if nowhere else, that he is no greater than the poor man, and the poor man should receive visible consolation that we are all equal in the sight of God."

In 1818, the same year that he presented Stralsund's councillors with his proposals for the Marienkirche, Friedrich married Caroline Bommer. To judge from her letters, she was a cheerful, humorous Saxon woman whose destiny, like that of her female contemporaries, lay in the narrow confines of a housewife's existence – something already hinted at in the painting *Woman at the Window* (ill. p. 14). Other than that, we know very little about her. She was 25 when she married the 44-year-old Friedrich, who in his letters always addressed her as "Line". Whether she was the sister of the supplier from whom Friedrich obtained his pencils, or whether the artist spotted her in one of the *tableaux vivants* frequently staged by artists in those days, as Carus noted, or whether he met her through Kersting, to whom she was related, are questions that must remain open. Later on, Friedrich is said to have been consumed by enormous – unfounded – jealousy and to have harangued her on occasions out of spite, but whether that is true also remains uncertain. "It's a droll business, when a fellow has a wife," wrote Friedrich, as he observed how marriage had profoundly changed his former bachelor existence. He had to equip the house from top to bottom and buy cupboards, tables, chairs

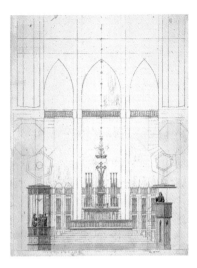

Overall View of the Proposed Renovation of the Choir, Marienkirche, Stralsund, 1817
Grey and brown pen and grey wash,
60.4 x 39.2 cm
Nuremberg, Germanisches Nationalmuseum

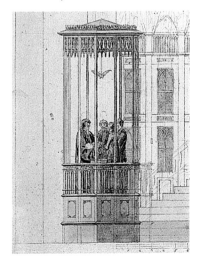

Detail from *Overall View of the Proposed Renovation of the Choir*

and a "bed of sin", as he states in one passage of a letter that is often passed over.
But all of these things, he emphasizes in his writings, were obligations that he
was happy to fulfil.

That Caroline was a positive influence is evidenced not least by the fact that,
from this point on, women appear with greater frequency in his work. A new,
friendly element seems to enter his pictures. A case in point is the painting to which
some authors give the title *Woman before the Rising Sun*, and which others call
Woman before the Setting Sun, which was painted around 1818–1820. The woman
seen in rear view appears as a large silhouette against the intense reddish-yellow
of the sky. It is difficult to interpret the fervent gesture of her outstretched arms
and the stylized rays radiating from the mountains on the hazy horizon, herald-
ing the presence of the invisible sun. Caroline was probably the model for the
female figure in old-German dress. Since she is stepping towards the light like an
early Christian in prayer, some have sought to interpret the painting in terms of
a communion with nature. Friedrich may have drawn inspiration for this motif
from paintings and engravings of the 18th century, in particular works in the
Protestant and Calvinist tradition, in which comparable figures are portrayed
bathing in the morning light. On the other hand, the atmosphere evoked in Friedrich's painting might be interpreted as that of dusk, the path which terminates
so abruptly as an announcement of death, and the boulders scattered alongside
the path as symbols of faith. In the final analysis, few of Friedrich's pictures are
as emphatic and almost exaggeratedly symbolic in their effect – factors which
render the painting not unproblematic for the viewer.

Similarly impressive, but much more straightforward in tone, is the St Petersburg painting *On the Sailing Boat*, completed around 1819 (ill. p. 50). The future
Tsar Nicholas I probably purchased the painting in 1820, when he visited Friedrich in his Dresden studio. As if we ourselves were on board, our eyes are directed
towards the prow of the boat, where a couple are sitting. They are holding hands
and gazing at the distant city ahead, its church spires and buildings emerging
hazily from the mist. A new destination? A return home? The woman is once
again Caroline, and the man is probably intended to be Friedrich. The artist is

possibly referring here to the motif of the ship of life, to the notion of life as a journey from this world to the next, as familiar from Christian pictorial and literary tradition, and perhaps even to the demand for political freedom – the man is wearing old-German dress, whose significance in Friedrich's pictures will be discussed further below (cf. pp. 56f.). The picture is dominated, however, by the emotional span between the narrowness of the boat, the way in which it seems to be gliding soundlessly forwards, strangely without waves, and the longed-for horizon. Dominant, too, is the bold composition with its slightly offset verticals (the mast), its horizontals (the distant shore) and its foreshortened view of the wedge-like front of the ship. It would be several decades before a close-up view of this kind would be encountered again in the work of the Impressionists.

The Chalk Cliffs on Rügen (ill. p. 53) ranks as one of Friedrich's most beautiful paintings. Executed during Friedrich's honeymoon in the summer of 1818, it portrays the Stubbenkammer cliffs, one of the most popular destinations on the island of Rügen. A grassy strip of solid ground in the foreground describes a sweeping curve between the trees on either side of the painting, almost bisecting the lower edge of the picture a little left of the central vertical. Meeting in a V at precisely this most dangerous point in the picture are the chalk cliffs which rise, along with a sense of bottomless depth, out of the abyss below. As if through a window, we look out between the chalk walls and across the bizarre silhouettes of a number of chalk pinnacles into the distance, at the infinite vastness of the ocean, whose surface, with its bands of greyish to pinkish blue, demonstrates a different kind of immaterial fathomlessness. These parts of the canvas then evaporate into the ethereal dimension of the limpid, reddish sky above. The woman and the two men occupying their bold vantage point in the foreground can be understood in very different ways. Amongst the numerous interpretations that have been put forward, the most convincing is the suggestion that the painting represents an allegory of Friedrich's love for his wife and falls into the tradition of Romantic friendship paintings, as indicated by the heart-shaped form of the internal frame described by the grassy ground and the trees. The standing figure in old-German dress on the right might thereby represent the artist himself in his idealized youth, directing his gaze towards infinity and the two sailing boats, which probably symbolize his own and his wife's ships of life. The elderly man in the middle, crawling towards the edge of the cliff like some strange reptile, could be a second Friedrich, now a figure of doubt who wants to ascertain, cautiously and fearfully, whether there is indeed something alluring to be found down in the direction where the women is pointing.

In whichever way the painting is interpreted, one thing is certain: Friedrich is here confronting near and far, comparing them with one another and thereby heightening their respective effect. The artist and his wife, on a honeymoon which has expanded into their life's journey, have climbed up to a lookout point which demands an even more courageous excursion: on the one hand, into one's own self, and on the other hand, beyond present and future into a hereafter. The eye comprehends the message conveyed by the ships – a lengthy voyage, a taking leave of the narrow shores of the present and the familiar and a setting sail for the never-ending promise and hope offered by the far horizon. It is for this reason that the figures have scrambled this far and brought the viewer with them to this exposed spot, where their walk transforms itself into a transcendental experience, during which all they now see between the trees and the cliffs are sea and sky.

Out of a most profound mistrust of authority, as Friedrich wrote to his brother Christian in 1817, and in the wake of his marriage, which brought with it a new

Chalk Cliffs on Rügen, 1818
Oil on canvas, 90.5 x 71 cm
Winterthur, Oskar Reinhart foundation

This painting, which numbers amongst Friedrich's most famous works, arose during his honeymoon in the summer of 1818. It depicts the Stubbenkammer cliffs, one of the most popular vantage points on the island of Rügen.

emphasis upon intimacy, the artist now devoted increasing energy to his private, personal relationships. He continued to stay in touch, through visits, with Kersting, who was now living in Meissen; indeed, since Kersting was related to Friedrich's wife Caroline, their contact may even have intensified. His friendship with Carus began in 1818 and at times seems to have been very close. It was in 1818, too, that the Norwegian artist Dahl moved to Dresden and quickly made Friedrich's acquaintance. In 1823 he moved into the third floor of "An der Elbe33", the house in which Friedrich had been living with his family since 1820. For Caspar David, who although melancholy in character was by no means averse to a sophisticated joke, the easy-going and cheerful Dahl must have made a pleasant lodger, one for whom he was happy to fetch an extra chair so that the two could sit in his studio and chat. Their artistic association was also extremely fruitful. Friedrich's private life was not untouched by grief, however. When one of his closest friends, the painter Gerhard von Kügelgen, who had been living in Dresden since 1805 and had been a professor at the Academy there since 1814, was murdered while out for a walk, this dreadful event plunged Friedrich into a deep and long-lasting depression.

The Tree of Crows, c. 1822
Oil on canvas, 54 x 71 cm
Paris, Musée du Louvre

The hillock in the centre of the composition probably represents one of the dolmens on Rügen; the island's steep shoreline and long, narrow ridge running far out into the sea are visible in the left-hand background.

Not only did Friedrich become more sociable during this period of his life, but he even decided to give private tuition to a number of pupils. This would have been unthinkable earlier, for this was an artist who had emphatically declared: "Is there not an enormous narrow-mindedness and arrogance to the belief that one can and may burden young people with one's views and opinions?" A new pleasure in the company of sympathetic friends now helped Friedrich to overcome such pedagogical scruples. From this point onwards, people assume a more prominent role in his pictures and become considerably larger. Figures also appear more frequently in pairs closely bound by friendship or love, etching themselves forever on the memory in images of supreme potency, such as *Evening Landscape with Two Men* of c. 1830–1835. One of the most beautiful examples of such paintings of two figures is *Two Men Contemplating the Moon* (ill. p. 56), which arose around 1819/20. According to some sources, the man on the right is Friedrich himself, with his pupil August Heinrich beside him. According to Dahl, however, the two figures represent Friedrich's brother-in-law and pupil Christian Wilhelm Bommer and August Heinrich. The men are standing in a rugged rocky landscape beneath an evergreen spruce, symbol of permanence. The dead oak tree with its roots laid bare which is threatening to topple over on

Evening Landscape with Two Men,
c. 1830–1835
Oil on canvas, 25 x 31 cm
St Petersburg, Hermitage Museum

the right might represent the state of Germany during the repressive era which followed the Congress of Vienna. Friedrich took up the motif again, in slightly varied form, in the painting *Man and Woman Contemplating the Moon* (ill. p. 57), in which he has perhaps portrayed himself and his wife in this scene of Romantic wonderment.

In each of these pictures, the men are wearing the old-German costume which appears in Friedrich's œuvre from about 1815 onwards: a grey or black coat buttoned up to the neck, a wide shirt collar and a black velvet biretta worn over – in most cases – shoulder-length hair. Arndt had propagated this style of dress during the Wars of Liberation, and it was subsequently adopted by volunteers with the Lützower *Freikorps* and later by members of the *Burschenschaften*, the associations of militant students which formed at Germany's universities. Although the wearing of the politically-charged old-German costume was forbidden under the new regime, even during these years of severe censorship Friedrich never banished it from his pictures, even those – and indeed, especially not those – portraying his close friends. In 1820 he observed laconically of the two men contemplating the moon: "They're plotting demagogic intrigues." In the case of Friedrich, looking back to the past is never an exercise in pure nostalgia; in the revolutionary spirit of Early Romanticism, it also implies looking into the future.

Two Men Contemplating the Moon, c. 1819/20
Oil on canvas, 35 x 44 cm
Dresden, Gemäldegalerie Neue Meister, Staatliche Kunstsammlungen Dresden

In response to demand from his clientele, Friedrich executed several copies of this composition, a number of which remain in private collections.

Man and Woman Contemplating the Moon,
c. 1824
Oil on canvas, 34 x 44 cm
Berlin, Nationalgalerie, Staatliche Museen
zu Berlin – Preussischer Kulturbesitz

In this painting, Friedrich has probably portrayed himself and his wife gazing at the moon
in Romantic wonderment.

Old-German dress is also worn by the protagonist in the famous *Wanderer
above a Sea of Mist* of 1818 (ill. p. 58). On top of a dark outcrop of rock, rising
steeply in the foreground, stands a man seen in rear view. He is gazing across the
sea of mist rising from the valley, past the naked pillars of rock emerging here and
there into the clear air, and out towards the peaks and mountain ranges in the distance. A bank of clouds lies high above. At the heart of the painting undoubtedly
lies the evocation of the sublime, as formulated by Carus in 1835: "Climb up, then,
to the summit of the mountain, gaze out over the long chains of hills … and
with what emotion are you seized? – You are filled with silent devotion, you lose
yourself in boundless space, your whole being undergoes a quiet cleansing and
purification, your ego-self vanishes, you are nothing, God is all." Friedrich's rear-
view figure is in all probability intended as a patriotic monument to one who has
died. The mist illustrates the cycle of nature. We should remember in this context
the ideas of Jean-Jacques Rousseau, who in the middle of the 18th century described the purifying effect of the high mountains as the place closest to the ether,
the fabric of the highest heaven, the fifth element or *quinta essentia*. Friedrich's
"wanderer of the world" is also looking beyond the mist and mountain peaks into
ethereal realms, into the divine quintessence that brings peace to all. The rear-view
figure, so typical of Friedrich's work, thereby serves as a vehicle of meaning within

The Wanderer above a Sea of Mist, c. 1818
Oil on canvas, 98.4 x 74.8 cm
Hamburg, Hamburger Kunsthalle

"… it was a picture of the kind that only an aeronaut can see, when he rises in his airship above
the height of the clouds … up to where … the untroubled blue of the heaven is visible between
the wisps of mist." Thus Gotthilf Heinrich von Schubert, writing on this painting in 1855.

Hutten's Tomb, c. 1823/24
Oil on canvas, 93 x 73 cm
Weimar, Staatliche Kunstsammlungen

Engraved on the pedestal supporting the armour is the name "Hutten", while the inscriptions "Jahn 1813", "Arndt 1813", "Stein 1813", "Görres 1821", "D … 1821" and "F. Scharnhorst" can be made out on the front end of the sarcophagus. The painting represents an overt declaration of the artist's allegiance to the ideals of the Wars of Liberation and German nationalism.

the composition and at the same time mediates between the viewer and the painting, both in formal terms and with regard to its underlying layers of meaning.

Friedrich's desire for religious and political renewal (both are fundamentally inseparable) never really waned. Related motifs from his earlier years were later taken up again and restated in emphatic terms. One such is his *Vision of the Christian Church* (ill. p. 60), probably c. 1820, opinions of whose artistic merit are highly mixed. Another is *Dolmen in Autumn* from approximately the same period, and the portrait-format *Hutten's Tomb* (c. 1823/24; ill. p. 59). This last painting represents a memorial to the humanist and knight Ulrich von Hutten (1488–1523), a contemporary of Luther who was forced to flee his native Germany. Even if, by the early 19th century, the precise location of his final resting-place was no longer known (he was in fact buried on the island of Ufenau in Lake Zurich), Friedrich's vision of *Hutten's Tomb* represents a more than loud declaration of the artist's allegiance to the ideals of the Wars of Liberation and German nationalism. The medieval architecture providing the backdrop to *The Sisters on the Balcony* (ill. p. 62), is perhaps also intended to invoke the national pride associated with the neo-Gothic style. Pessimistic in mood, by contrast, is *The Tree of Crows* (ill. p. 54) of c. 1822 in the Louvre, a painting founded upon strong colour contrasts. The hillock in the centre of the composition probably represents one of the dolmens on Rügen; the island's bluffs and long, narrow reef running far out into the sea are visible in the left-hand background. The bare oak tree with its bizarrely twisted branches goes back to studies made considerably earlier in Friedrich's career. In contrast to the ravaged trees around it, it obstinately stands up to every storm. A striking note within the painting is sounded by the red of the stumps and tree debris, which together with the crows or ravens announce disaster and death.

Having barely changed at all right into the 1820s, Friedrich's style now began to show signs of a subtle evolution. His formerly somewhat reserved, dry, often monochrome use of colour now began to give way to a more differentiated palette. Passages of glaze are complemented by areas of impasto; the colour range is frequently enhanced with very light values, and Friedrich's handling of paint becomes looser

PAGE 63 TOP:
Evening, c. 1824
Oil on cardboard, 20 x 27.5 cm
Mannheim, Kunsthalle

PAGE 63 BOTTOM:
Drifting Clouds, c. 1820
Oil on canvas, 18.3 x 24.5 cm
Hamburg, Hamburger Kunsthalle

This small composition is probably identical to a
work recorded in Dresden in 1859 and described
as portraying a Riesengebirge landscape with
the source of the Elbe.

The Sisters on the Balcony, c. 1820
Oil on canvas, 74 x 52 cm
St Petersburg, The Hermitage

The Gothic cityscape combines buildings from
Halle, Stralsund, Neubrandenburg and Greifswald. The two women in old-German costume
may be Friedrich's wife Caroline and his sister-
in-law Elisabeth.

and somewhat more spontaneous. These changes may have been inspired by Dahl,
who had seen works by the English landscape painter John Constable (1776–1837)
on show in Paris. English influences, whether from Constable or others working
in a similar vein, may also account for Friedrich's interest in cloud studies during
this period, as evidenced by *Evening* (ill. p.63) of 1824, a small oil study on cardboard which is highly innovative, almost avant-garde in character. Goethe, having
admired Friedrich's work at first hand in 1810, had invited him in 1816 to illustrate
his meteorological studies. When Friedrich declined to reduce his emotionally-
coloured portrayal of clouds and cloud imagery to a scientific system, the two
men fell out. Friedrich's more forceful cloud formations are thus the result of his
own reflections and aims. Whether layers of symbolism lie hidden behind such
seemingly fleeting moments – as captured, for example, in *Drifting Clouds* of
c. 1820/21 (ill. p.63) – is a question that must on the whole remain unanswered.

Morning, 1821
Oil on canvas, 22 x 30.5 cm
Hanover, Niedersächsisches Landesmuseum

The four small pictures in Hanover (cf. also ills.
pp. 66–67) comprise one of Friedrich's best-known
cycles of the times of day.

The artists of Romanticism frequently conceived their subjects in terms of cycles. Around 1820, Friedrich commenced one of his best-known cycles of the times of day for the Halberstadt collector Dr Wilhelm Körte. *Morning* and *Evening* (ills. pp. 64/65, 67) were followed one year later by *Midday* and *Afternoon* (ill. p. 66, 67). Diverging in palette but similar in format, the paintings at first sight appear to be portraying simply the changing moods of the landscape at different times of the day. Just how much further Friedrich is looking beyond the pure phenomenon itself, however, emerges from one of his diary entries. In this case, it is the seasons whose changing appearances strike an inner chord in the artist and which ultimately, in the case of winter, conjure up for him an image of *vanitas* and death. "Today for the first time the normally so glorious countryside cries out to me of decay and death, where before it has only smiled to me of joy and life. The sky is overcast and stormy, and today it casts its monochrome winter coat over the lovely coloured mountains and fields for the first time. All nature lies before me drained of colour." Friedrich's experience of the landscape immediately before him is blended in his memory and imagination with other similar experiences. What he notes down in his diary as his emotionally and spiritually-charged reaction to real impressions, he composes in his painting into a grand cycle of natural destiny. The expressive characters of each landscape thereby fuse, within the overall impression of the cycle as a whole, into a world order characterized by growth and decay – just as the final picture in the series leads back into the first.

PAGE 67 TOP:
Afternoon, 1822
Oil on canvas, 22 x 31 cm
Hanover, Niedersächsisches Landesmuseum

PAGE 67 BOTTOM:
Evening, 1820/21
Oil on canvas, 22.3 x 31 cm
Hanover, Niedersächsisches Landesmuseum

Midday, 1822
Oil on canvas, 22 x 30 cm
Hanover, Niedersächsisches Landesmuseum

"Dusk was his element"

"Dusk was his element" – thus wrote Carus in his obituary of Friedrich, and thereby pointed to one of the cardinal themes in his art: morning and evening, rise and fall, growth and decay, birth and death – in other words, the elementary cycles of life. But Carus' words can also be taken to mean that Friedrich's late work took on a nocturnal, pessimistic slant, even if expressed in increasingly monumental form and in grand, artistically sovereign gestures. The old spirit of resistance, the utopian impulse nevertheless emerges not infrequently even here, and issues a defiant rebuttal to the hopeless circumstances of the time. Although the 1820s and 1830s may be understood as a relatively experimental phase in Friedrich's œuvre, they by no means represent a break with the past. Just as they saw him taking up new ideas, they also saw him continuing to pursue earlier ideals which remained dear to his heart.

When Friedrich's son Adolf expressed the desire to become a painter, Caspar David responded: "It's always said there's no money in art, but many people earn a living by it, some of them very handsomely." Friedrich may not have numbered amongst these last, but nor, in the 1820s, was he badly off. He submitted new works fairly regularly to the art exhibitions at home in Dresden and further afield in Hamburg, Königsberg (modern Kaliningrad) and Prague. Many art critics and art journals continued to review his works favourably. In their gauzy, atmospheric transparency, paintings such as *Meadows near Greifswald* (ill. p. 71), probably executed soon after 1820, and *Boat on the River Elbe in the Early Morning Mist* (ill. p. 70) from around the same period, offer the public – beyond all possible symbolism – an undisputed feast for the eyes. Two compositions in a similar vein to the *Boat on the River Elbe* were included in the Dresden Academy exhibitions of 1821 and 1822. The Berlin publisher and book-seller Georg Andreas Reimer, who had been born in Greifswald and who shared Friedrich's political convictions, built up a large collection of the artist's paintings.

In the 1820s and 1830s, the Russian court also purchased a number of works by Friedrich at the suggestion of the poet and state councillor Zhukovsky. These included the beautiful, large-format *Moonrise by the Sea*, which is dated fairly unanimously to around 1821 (ill. p. 74). Carus, Friedrich's friend and artist colleague, once asked Friedrich to show him how to paint moonlight. "He recommended that I take a dark glaze on my palette and lay it over everything except the moon and the luminous areas around it, and the nearer the edge the darker,

Johan Christian Clausen Dahl
Landscape with Rocky Fortress and Waterfall,
1819
Oil on canvas, 53.5 x 65 cm
Bergen, Billedgalleri Bergen

Rocky Ravine, c. 1822/23
Oil on canvas, 94 x 74 cm
Vienna, Kunsthistorisches Museum

The sandstone formation in the background stands on the Neurathen in the Elbsandstein-gebirge mountains. The rocks are portrayed larger than in real life, and Friedrich has introduced a deep ravine beneath the tallest pinnacle.

**Boat on the River Elbe in the Early Morning
Mist,** c. 1820. Oil on canvas, 22.5 x 30.8 cm
Cologne, Wallraf-Richartz-Museum

Carl Gustav Carus
Moonlit Night near Rügen, c. 1819
Oil on canvas, 38 x 47.5 cm. Dresden, Gemälde-
galerie Alte Meister, Staatliche Kunstsammlungen

The disc of the moon which, in Friedrich's work,
radiates a powerful luminosity and stands as a
mysterious sign in the sky, has in Carus's painting become a realistic atmospheric phenomenon.

and then to take note of how this changed the effect." The moon in the St Petersburg painting has been interpreted as Christ, the ships as symbols of approaching death and the anchor as a sign of the hope of resurrection. A contemporary
description is considerably more reserved, venturing only to say that two men
have clambered across the rocks a long way out into the shallows and appear to
be waiting for a ship. Their two female companions are seated more in the foreground. Two massive anchors take the place of vegetation, which is here reduced
simply to some saltwater plants.

The exceptionally large *Morning in the Mountains* (ill. p. 72), which probably
dates from around 1822/23, also went to St Petersburg. Its vast panorama has often
been interpreted as a vision of the hereafter, although the pastoral staffage in the
foreground lends the whole the quality of an idyll and the rocky terrain can in
fact be accessed via the path that runs at least as far as the steep cliffs in the middle ground. Opening up in front of the tiny shepherds on the rocky pinnacle, so
we assume, is a view down into the dizzying depths below and beyond the track
and cliffs into the infinite distance – a view yielding an impression of the sublime. Such emotionally saturated imagery, the visual language of atmospheric
and "ideal" painting alike, stood in blunt contradiction to the Realist tendencies
emerging in Germany at that time, as seen above all in the work of the Düsseldorf School. Friedrich emphatically rejected pure fidelity to life, the mere imitation of what was perceived by the human eye, since "art must issue from man's

interior, and depends on his moral and religious worth." Only on a few occasions does Friedrich appear to have attempted a more realistic approach, as for example in the unusually dramatic *Rocky Ravine* of c. 1822/23 (ill. p. 68). Untamed nature is here portrayed with a descriptive detail that betrays the influence of Friedrich's fellow artist Dahl, who had specialized in precisely such a style.

The painting *Village Landscape in Morning Light (The Lone Tree)* (ill. p. 73), which can be dated to 1822, also seems fairly realistic at first sight. The composition is not the product of a single, specific visual impression, however, but is highly artificial, being composed of no less than six individual studies which Friedrich executed between 1806 and 1810. The landscape-format composition presents a plain extending without interruption into the background, seen as if the viewer were standing on the gentle rise which begins in the bottom left and right-hand corners. From here, our gaze falls upon a small pond – to which no path leads – and upon a huge oak tree, which looks at first sight to be fairly close by. Once our eyes have also registered the diminutive figure of a shepherd leaning against its trunk, however, the tree suddenly appears further away and hence gigantic. Aspects of proximity and distance are permanently chafing against each other throughout the painting, whereby rational everyday experience is thwarted by visual irrationality. While an idyll of unspoilt nature unfolds around the oak and the shepherd, the villages and church spires of the land developed by man are as it were concealed and compressed within a valley by the mountains

Meadows near Greifswald, c. 1822
Oil on canvas, 34.5 x 48.3 cm
Hamburg, Hamburger Kunsthalle

Friedrich's native town becomes a symbol of longing for a better world. The prancing horses, the geese and the pond reflecting the sky reinforce the sense of idyll.

and the sky high above. All this points to an overall symbolism in which the oak tree, monumentalized to the status of protagonist, is a metaphor for growth and decay or for human life in general; where man entrusts himself to such elementals, as the shepherd has done, he is able to establish harmony and peace.

The transcendental note struck by this painting is further amplified in its identically-sized pendant, the Berlin *Moonrise by the Sea* (ill. p. 75). Evening now replies to morning. The annual round subjugates humankind to its law. Distances can no longer be gauged in rational terms, so that water, ships, moon and sky open up a dream world extending between yearning and melancholy, between near and far, between this world and the universe. Looking becomes meditative contemplation. No wonder that Friedrich seemed, in the eyes of his contemporaries, to be drifting in such paintings into the realm of mysticism, into a fantasy world which many were no longer able or even willing to comprehend. In the 1820s, the new regime had extinguished the intellectual and artistic fire of Early Romanticism in Dresden. Friedrich, now politically out of favour, would come to feel the change in climate at first hand. When the chair in landscape painting became vacant at the Academy in 1824, Friedrich should have been the

Morning in the Mountains, c. 1822/23
Oil on canvas, 135 x 170 cm
St Petersburg, The Hermitage

This large-format painting was probably purchased by the future Alexander II of Russia, whose collection also included *Moonrise by the Sea* (ill. p. 74).

obvious candidate. But he was denied the post, on the awkward grounds that the inner compulsion of his genius, rather than thorough study, had made him the artist he was, and that he was therefore unsuited to teaching. By way of consolation, he was at least appointed an associate professor, albeit without a class of students.

That same year produced a painting which may be understood as a sort of programmatic statement and résumé of Friedrich's aims and intentions. *The Sea of Ice* (ill. p. 76/77) is undoubtedly one of the artist's masterpieces, yet the radical nature of its composition and subject was greeted in its own day with incomprehension and rejection. It was disparagingly dismissed as "tedious" : "If only the ice painting of the North Pole would melt once and for all," wished one of its contemptuous critics. The picture remained unsold right up to Friedrich's death in 1840. In 1905 it was purchased by the Hamburger Kunsthalle from the estate of the heirs of Friedrich's Norwegian colleague and friend, Dahl. The sailing ship being slowly crushed by pack ice in a polar landscape otherwise devoid of signs of human life may be understood as a pathos-laden metaphor for a catastrophe on an epochal scale, whereby visually coded references to ruin and nevertheless to hope, to destruction and to regeneration, combine into a symbolic protest against the oppressive "political winter" gripping Germany under Metternich.

Village Landscape in Morning Light (The Lone Tree), 1822
Oil on canvas, 55 x 71 cm
Berlin, Nationalgalerie, Staatliche Museen zu Berlin – Preussischer Kulturbesitz

A source of inspiration for the painting was the polar expedition mounted by William Edward Parry from 1819 to 1820 in search of the North-west Passage. The fascinating picture, its icy palette corresponding to the Arctic setting, also contains an echo of that dreadful episode in Friedrich's childhood when his young brother fell through the ice and drowned, a tragedy partly precipitated by Friedrich himself. Although the sea has turned to solid ice and organic nature, like the ship, is condemned to death, the light-filled sky and the boundless horizon symbolize, as so often in Friedrich's work, the chance of salvation. In reply to the slabs of ice in the foreground, rising to form a sharp-edged, fissured pyramid and gathering within themselves the forces of final destruction, the seemingly weightless and transparent background exudes a solemn calm. Two fragments of ice configured in the shape of an arrow point to the stranded ship. In marrying the terrible with the sublime, the polar world is transformed into a vessel of human emotions. Closely related to *The Sea of Ice* and probably executed only shortly afterwards is *Rocky Reef on the Sea Shore* (ill. p. 78), which probably depicts the western tip of the Isle of Wight off Bournemouth, a view which Friedrich may have known from engravings. The rocky needles in the sea recall the ice formations in the Hamburg painting.

Moonrise by the Sea, c. 1821
Oil on canvas, 135 x 170 cm
St Petersburg, The Hermitage

1824 was a particularly fruitful year for the artist, but also an exhausting one. He had overworked himself, and developed a complaint to which he refers in only vague terms in a letter of 21 October 1825, addressed to his three brothers Adolf, Heinrich and Christian in Greifswald: "I have been unwell for a while, but since yesterday my illness seems to be on the retreat. I have just wrapped myself up in furs and sat down at my desk in order to spend the day conversing with you. I have the need from time to time, my dear brothers, to repeat to you how very much I love you and how unbounded is my trust in you, the more my painful experiences cause me to withdraw into myself. But don't let my words give you cause for concern…" Between now and 1826, his illness prevented him from working much in oil. Instead, he produced chiefly drawings and water-colours of Rügen, which were to be reproduced as engravings and provide a collection of views of the island. One of the most striking of these sheets is the 1826 sepia drawing *Sunrise over the Sea* (ill. p. 79), in which the sea is portrayed as an absorbing primal element, as it were, from which the sun, with its symmetrical rays, rises and casts its light over the crests of the unending waves. There is no beach, no shoreline, no ship to define the viewer's position. In an eminently modern fashion, Friedrich reduces his composition to the simplest pictorial

Moonrise by the Sea, c. 1822
Oil on canvas, 55 x 71 cm
Berlin, Nationalgalerie, Staatliche Museen
zu Berlin – Preussischer Kulturbesitz

This painting is the pendant to *Village Land-scape in Morning Light* (ill. p. 73). The horizon, which falls across the canvas at almost exactly mid-height, separates two hyperbolic curves (one described by the line of the clouds, the other by the silhouette of the rocks on the shore), which mirror each other in a composi-tional structure typical of Friedrich.

The Sea of Ice, c. 1823/24
Oil on canvas, 96.7 x 126.9 cm
Hamburg, Hamburger Kunsthalle

The painting may be understood as a programmatic statement and résumé of Friedrich's aims
and intentions. It can rightly be called one of the
key paintings of the 19th century.

Rocky Reef on the Sea Shore, c. 1824
Oil on canvas, 22 x 31 cm
Karlsruhe, Staatliche Kunsthalle

means of geometry, colour and light – elements identical to those of the subject being portrayed. Precursors of this radical pictorial form can be found in engravings of the 16th and 17th centuries, which visualize the creation of Light on the first day of Creation in a comparable fashion, although they also include the figure of God the Father or a symbol of the Trinity.

When Friedrich resumed working in oil following the provisional end of his illness, there lingered a dark shadow which also afflicted his private life – a forewarning of the stroke he would later suffer and which would hasten his death. The motif of the graveyard now began to appear with greater frequency in his œuvre, as for example in the painting *The Cemetery Entrance* (ill. p. 80), which was probably commenced in 1825 but which remained unfinished. The imposing gateway is based on that of the Trinitatis cemetery in Dresden. Above the open child's grave in the foreground are the thin, barely visible outlines of hovering figures, and in the middle of the entrance an angel with outstretched arms. The two figures leaning against the pillar on the left are the grieving parents. The same symbolic and heavy sadness lies over *The Cemetery Gate* of c. 1825–1830 today in Bremen (ill. p. 81) and the Leipzig *Graveyard under Snow* of 1826 (ill. p. 82). In the latter picture, the view is reversed: we are now looking from inside the cemetery across the grave to the open gate, which is surrounded by a latticework of bare branches. The stormy sky is dead and empty. Paintings such as *Hut under Snow*, today to be seen in the Nationalgalerie in Berlin,

depicting a hayrick buried under snow and bare willows, and *Early Snow*, today in the Hamburger Kunsthalle, also share the general mood of transitoriness and death.

In the latter part of the 1820s, Friedrich began taking up motifs which had previously served as parts of a larger landscape tableau and restating them as absolutes in a new and magnified form. A typical example is his *Oak Tree in Snow*, executed around 1829 (ill. p. 83). Oak trees are encountered, like a leitmotif, throughout Friedrich's œuvre, often in conjunction with a dolmen. They are a personal reminder for the artist of his native roots and are at the same time charged with nationalist sentiment. The tree in the Berlin picture – a slightly different version is housed in the Wallraf-Richartz-Museum in Cologne – is positively defiant, rising in portrait format against a steely blue sky. For all the stumpiness of its limbs, it is an exclamation mark placed against winter and death.

Around 1830 Friedrich increasingly began to shut himself off from the world, withdrawing ever deeper into his tortured self. He had finally come to realise, moreover, that his art no longer had anything to say to anyone but his closest friends and initiates. He made a virtue of his isolation when he wrote: "It may be a great honour to have a large public on one's side. But it is surely a much greater honour to have a small, select public on one's side." In a pun on the German words allgemein (common in the sense of general) and gemein (common in the sense of coarse or vulgar), he went on: "To be commonly pleasing

Sunrise over the Sea, 1826
Sepia over pencil, 18.7 x 26.6 cm
Hamburg, Hamburger Kunsthalle

The sheet forms one of a series of seven drawings symbolizing the stages of life. Precursors of this radical pictorial form can be found in engravings of the 16th and 17th centuries, which visualize the creation of Light on the first day of Creation in a comparable fashion.

The Cemetery Entrance, 1825
Oil on canvas, 143 x 110 cm
Dresden, Gemäldegalerie Neue Meister,
Staatliche Kunstsammlungen Dresden

The Cemetery Gate (The Churchyard), c. 1825–1830
Oil on canvas, 31 x 25.2 cm
Bremen, Kunsthalle Bremen

At an exhibition mounted by the Bremer Kunst-Verein in 1833, the
painting bore the title *Priessnitz Churchyard near Dresden*. Friedrich
and Dahl are known to have made drawings of this cemetery in 1824.

Graveyard under Snow, 1826
Oil on canvas, 31 x 25.3 cm
Leipzig, Museum der bildenden Künste,
Maximilian Speck von Sternberg Foundation

The open grave in the foreground has prompted much speculation.
Some have suggested that it is intended as the future resting-place of the artist.

Oak Tree in Snow, c. 1829
Oil on canvas, 71 x 48 cm
Berlin, Nationalgalerie, Staatliche Museen zu Berlin – Preussischer Kulturbesitz

Oak trees run like a leitmotif throughout Friedrich's œuvre, often in
conjunction with a dolmen. They are a reminder of the artist's personal
roots and are at the same time charged with nationalist sentiment.

Landscape with Grave, Coffin and Owl,
c. 1836/37
Sepia over pencil, 38.5 x 38.3 cm
Hamburg, Hamburger Kunsthalle

Visible in the background is Cape Arkona on the
island of Rügen, although in a different landscape setting. It is possible that the owl, while
undoubtedly a bird of death, here also represents
a symbol of wisdom.

PAGE 85 TOP:
The Watzmann, c. 1824/25
Oil on canvas, 135 x 170 cm
Berlin, Nationalgalerie, Staatliche Museen
zu Berlin – Preussischer Kulturbesitz

Despite its apparent fidelity to nature, the painting reveals a somewhat fantastical element in its
mixture of different geological formations and
its unnatural ratios of scale.

PAGE 85 BOTTOM:
Adrian Ludwig Richter
The Watzmann, 1824
Oil on canvas, 120.2 x 93 cm
Munich, Bayerische Staatsgemäldesammlungen,
Neue Pinakothek

means to please the common. Only the common (das Gemeine) is common (allgemein)."

Throughout his life, Friedrich demonstrated himself to be closely attached to his home. His numerous trips and walking tours to central Germany, Silesia, Bohemia, Greifswald, Neubrandenburg and Rügen never actually took him very far away. He never visited southern Germany, for example, and his painting of *The Watzmann* – a mountain near Berchtesgaden, portrayed here rising like a Gothic cathedral in its stone majesty – is based in Friedrich's words not on "autopsy", but was inspired by a watercolour by his pupil August Heinrich. It also rivalled a painting by Adrian Ludwig Richter of the same name, which went on show in Dresden in 1824 and was intended to back up Richter's application for the professorship in landscape painting at the Academy, the post to which Friedrich also aspired. Friedrich similarly executed a number of Swiss landscapes that were based entirely on sketches by his friend Carus. A reference to a supposed plan by Friedrich to visit Iceland in 1811 was probably also intended ironically. Most importantly of all, the artist never went to Italy, the land for which virtually every German artist of Romanticism and Late Romanticism yearned. All the more astonishing, therefore, is the painting *Temple of Juno in Agrigento*,

The Temple of Juno in Agrigent, c. 1830
Oil on canvas, 54 x 72 cm
Dortmund, Museum für Kunst und Kulturgeschichte
der Stadt Dortmund

Whether this painting should be attributed to Friedrich
or Carus still remains the subject of controversy. The
hardness of the line and the steep foreshortening of the
architecture are entirely untypical of Friedrich's œuvre.

Mountainous River Landscape (Day Version), c. 1830–1835
Mixed media on transparent paper, 76.8 x 127 cm
Kassel, Staatliche Museen Kassel

Mountainous River Landscape (Night Version), um 1830–1835
Mixed media on transparent paper, 76.8 x 127 cm
Kassel, Staatliche Museen Kassel

The Grosse Gehege near Dresden, c. 1832
Oil on canvas, 73.5 x 102.5 cm
Dresden, Gemäldegalerie Neue Meister,
Staatliche Kunstsammlungen Dresden

With the richness of its palette, the beauty of its
composition and its sonorous atmosphere, this
impressive painting is a true masterpiece in the
history of European landscape painting.

which can be dated to around 1830 (ill. p. 86). In view of the fact that it falls well
outside the usual scope of Friedrich's subject matter, this painting should perhaps be attributed to Carus. Whatever the case, Friedrich's focus throughout his
œuvre fell upon the marvellous in the near at hand – a focus frequently found in
German Romanticism and described by Ludwig Tieck in 1795 thus: "That which
is right around us we always judge to be everyday and boring; that which is to
delight us we seek far away." But: "The wonderful utopia often lies right at our
feet…" Friedrich clearly shied away from foreign travel and the prospect of a
wealth of experience which might have got out of his control and burdened him
with yearnings after his return. He nevertheless felt the longing for open air
shared by German artists in Rome and the Italian countryside, as an escape from
the "frosty" conditions prevailing in Germany during the Biedermeier period
leading up to the March Revolution of 1848 – conditions which inspired the sar-
castic title of Heinrich Heine's *Germany: A Winter's Tale.*

Friedrich's dreams led him in another direction, however. In 1830 he was
commissioned by Alexander, the heir to the Russian throne, to produce four
transparent pictures. Executed on transparent paper and lit from behind in a
dark room, the pictures would be viewed as an ensemble to the accompaniment
of music. In 1835 the four transparent pictures were dispatched to St Petersburg
together with the equipment needed to display them – sadly, they are now lost.
In Kassel, however, a similar example survives, a *Mountainous River Landscape*

Wreck in the Moonlight, c. 1835
Oil on canvas, 31.3 x 42.5 cm
Berlin, Nationalgalerie, Staatliche Museen
zu Berlin – Preussischer Kulturbesitz

painted on both sides of a single piece of transparent paper. When correctly lit, one side reveals itself to be a version of the composition seen in daylight, while the other side portrays the same scene at night (ills. p. 87). Such transparent pictures undoubtedly fall into the early history of entertainment media, of panoramas, indeed even of cinema.

After the political stagnation of the preceding years, in 1830 – in the wake of the July Revolution in France – things in Germany, and in Dresden, seemed to start moving again. This may have been one of the factors contributing to Friedrich's final phase of full mastery. Between 1830 and 1835 he produced such important works, full of inner maturity, as *The Stages of Life* discussed earlier (ill. p. 90/91). Another is *The Grosse Gehege near Dresden* (ill. p. 88), depicting an area of pastureland crossed by tree-lined avenues just outside Dresden, portrayed in masterly fashion from an alienating angle. Friedrich uses an exquisite palette to evoke a particularly solemn evening mood and thereby lends a rhythmic impulse to the foreground with rivulets of water glinting in the sunset. The modernity of his pictorial structure becomes clear in a comparison with the painting *Dunes* by Piet Mondrian (1872–1944), a work executed around 1911 and tending towards abstraction – even if no direct influence of the older master upon the younger can be proven. In the astonishing *Neubrandenburg in Flames* (ill. p. 92), Friedrich portrays a subject that possibly contains an apoca-

The Stages of Life, c. 1835
Oil on canvas, 73 x 94 cm
Leipzig, Museum der bildenden Künste

This painting, one of Friedrich's most famous
works, has been the subject of various interpretations. The suggestion that the five boats are
assigned to the five figures as symbols of life,
between departure and death, seems the most
convincing.

Neubrandenburg in Flames (Sunrise near Neubrandenburg), um 1835
Oil on canvas, 72.2 x 101.3 cm
Hamburg, Hamburger Kunsthalle

Clouds of smoke are billowing from windows and from the roof of the Marienkirche, part of which is missing. Flames even appear to be leaping from one of the windows. There are no records to say that this was an actual fire that Friedrich might have witnessed, however.

lyptic message. *Wreck in the Moonlight* (ill. p. 89) and *The Riesengebirge* (ill. p. 93), both executed around 1835, condense motifs typical of Friedrich into definitive statements which etch themselves indelibly upon the memory with their inner grandeur, their solemnity and their formal sovereignty.

On 26 June 1835 Friedrich suffered a stroke that left him partially paralysed in the arms and legs. After an initial period during which he was confined to bed, he went to Teplice to convalesce. He was from now on virtually unable to paint in oils and had to restrict himself to drawings. His sepia drawing *Landscape with Grave, Coffin and Owl* (ill. p. 84) is symptomatic of the obsession with which Friedrich tracked death in the last years of his life. The eyes of the exaggeratedly large, surreal night bird glint in the light of the moon which floats like a nimbus above the owl's head. The landscape is of "almost insane desolation" (Jens Christian Jensen). On 19 March 1840 Zhukovsky visited the artist in Dresden, by which time he had probably already suffered a second stroke. The Russian noted in his diary: "To Friedrich. Sad ruin. He wept like a child." Friedrich's greatest anxiety was that he might leave his family penniless. A few weeks later, on 7 May, he died. He was buried three days later in the Trinitatis cemetery in Dresden. Friedrich's godson and pupil, the painter Robert Kummer, gave the funeral address, and other friends and pupils made up the cortège.

Today Friedrich is celebrated as the masterly composer of stillness. He fashioned fleeting instants which embrace eternity and infinity and which capture a

momentary pause between growth and decay and between suffering and action. In 1834 the French sculptor David d'Angers (1788–1856) recognized in Friedrich the artist who had discovered "the tragedy of landscape". In 1889 Vincent van Gogh (1853–1890) sketched the *Window of Vincent's Studio in St Paul's Hospital* (today to be seen in Amsterdam at the Rijksmuseum Vincent van Gogh). When we compare this drawing with Friedrich's studio window of 1805/06 (ill. p. 8), we find ourselves catching our breath: in terms of both composition and the personal experience it reflects, the younger work seems to have been born entirely out of the spirit of the elder. But the possibility that van Gogh ever saw a work by Friedrich – whether in the original or as a reproduction – seems slim. Not so in the case of Gerhard Richter (b. 1932), one of the most important contemporary artists in Germany today. Richter's *Seascape* of 1975, for example, betrays a knowledge of the Romantic "painter of stillness", even if it is no longer rooted in a truly transcendental understanding of nature. The history of what, beyond superficial "Romanticisms", Friedrich's art had to give the 19th and 20th centuries, however, has yet to be written.

The Riesengebirge, c. 1835
Oil on canvas, 72 x 102 cm
Berlin, Nationalgalerie, Staatliche Museen
zu Berlin – Preussischer Kulturbesitz

Gerhard Richter
Seascape, 1975
Oil on canvas, 200 x 300 cm
Stuttgart, Froehlich Collection

Caspar David Friedrich 1774–1840
Chronology

Self-portrait with Cap and Sighting Eye-shield, 1802
Pencil, brush and ink, 17.5 x 10.5 cm
Hamburg, Hamburger Kunsthalle

1787 His brother Johann Christoffer drowns while trying to rescue Caspar David, who has fallen through the ice.

1788–1790 Caspar David's earliest artistic activity takes the form of calligraphic drawings on the pages of albums. These are followed by his first sketches. Around 1790, and perhaps as early as 1788, he takes lessons from Johann Gottfried Quistorp, the drawing master at Greifswald University, who teaches him architectural drawing and encourages him to experiment with the technique of etching.

1791 Friedrich's sister Maria dies of typhus.

1794 At the relatively late age of 20, Friedrich commences his studies in art at the Copenhagen Academy, where his most important teachers are Nicolai Abildgaard and in particular Jens Juel and Ch. A. Lorentzen. Friedrich has not yet committed himself to the genre of landscape painting; during this period he also illustrates scenes from Schiller's *Die Räuber* and other figural subjects.

1774 Caspar David is born in Greifswald, a small port and university town on the Baltic which until 1815 formed part of the kingdom of Sweden. He is the sixth child of the soap and candlemaker Adolf Gottlieb Friedrich and his wife Sophie Dorothea. The boy is soon confronted with death in his strictly Protestant family home.

1781 Friedrich's mother dies. A year later his sister Elisabeth dies of smallpox.

1798–1799 The artist returns to Greifswald, where he shows Quistorp the fruits of his studies and renews his acquaintance with Ernst Moritz Arndt, the future poet of German liberation. That same year he moves to Dresden, drawn to the city by its magnificent art collections and the beautiful countryside around it. In 1799 Friedrich takes part in the Dresden Academy art exhibition for the first time, showing a few drawings.

1801 Friedrich travels via Neubrandenburg to Greifswald, where he is visited

Mother Heiden, 1798 or c. 1801/02. Black chalk
Greifswald, Pommersches Landesmuseum

by Philipp Otto Runge. He makes a number of trips to the island of Rügen. Friedrich's personal style begins to emerge in his landscape drawings.

1805 Friedrich enjoys his first major success when he wins joint top prize with two sepia drawings in a competition organized by Johann Wolfgang von Goethe in Weimar.

1806 Napoleon conquers Prussia and Russia; Dresden is soon occupied.

1808 Friedrich attracts attention, acclaim and sharp criticism with *The Cross in the Mountains (The Tetschen Altar)*, which ignites the so-called Ramdohr Dispute. This same year, the first reading of Heinrich von Kleist's *Die Hermannsschlacht* (Hermann's Battle) probably takes place in Friedrich's studio. The painter's anti-French stance hardens; in conjunction with ideas of national liberation and religious renewal, it leads to a repertoire of symbolic motifs which will never again entirely disappear from Friedrich's œuvre.
These years are also filled with numerous trips and walking tours to Bohemia, Neubrandenburg, Greifswald and Rügen.

1809 Friedrich's father dies.

1810 *The Monk by the Sea* and *The Abbey in the Oak Wood* mark the start of what outwardly are probably the most successful years in Friedrich's career. He develops a method of composition that enables him to create some of the boldest and most innovative paintings of German Romanticism.

1814 Friedrich shows *The Chasseur in the Woods* at the Exhibition of Patriotic Art mounted in Dresden to celebrate the city's liberation.

Adolf Gottlieb Friedrich, Reading, 1802
Black chalk, 34.6 x 32 cm
Mannheim, Kunsthalle

1816 The artist is elected a member of the Dresden Academy, with a salary of 150 thalers. This encourages him to start thinking about marriage and children.

1818 In January Friedrich marries Caroline Bommer. This period sees him producing such important paintings as *The Wanderer above the Sea of Mist* and *Chalk Cliffs on Rügen*.

1819 The political situation worsens under the regime imposed by Metternich, and the Karlsbad Decrees usher in an era of censorship and the persecution of demagogues – events which deeply anger Friedrich. This same year his daughter Emma is born, followed in 1823 by a second daughter, Agnes Adelheid, and in 1824 by a son, Gustav Adolf.

1820 Friedrich is devastated by the murder of his dear friend and fellow artist Gerhard von Kügelgen. This same year, the Friedrich family moves to "An der Elbe 33", still in Dresden. In December Friedrich receives a high-ranking visitor: Grand Duke and future Tsar Nicholas I of Russia, who over the following years buys a number of paintings by the artist through the agency of the poet and state councillor Vasily Andreyevich Zhukovsky.

1823 The Norwegian Johan Christian Clausen Dahl, who also trained as a landscape painter at the Copenhagen Academy and who has been living in Dresden since 1818, moves into Friedrich's house. The friendship between the two men is also fruitful for their art, and they exhibit jointly in 1824, 1826, 1829 and 1833.

1824 Following the death of the incumbent professor, Johann Christian Klengel, the chair in landscape painting at the Dresden Academy becomes vacant. Friedrich is denied the post, however, probably for political reasons, and is made only an associate professor. In this year Friedrich paints one of his most striking pictures, *The Sea of Ice.*

1826–1828 Friedrich falls seriously ill and goes to Rügen to recuperate. For the time being he is virtually unable to paint in oils and is obliged to concentrate on drawings, which also brings financial problems. By 1828 his health appears to have improved.

Around 1830 Friedrich increasingly shuts himself off from the world, withdrawing ever deeper into his tortured self. He finally comes to realize that his art no longer has anything to say to anyone but his closest friends and initiates. In March 1830 he receives a visit from Crown Prince Frederick William of Prussia.
This same year, Friedrich writes with a mixture of sympathy and scepticism about the uprising in Dresden, which was inspired by the July Revolution in Paris.

1835 Friedrich suffers a stroke that leaves him partially paralysed in the arms and legs. Sales of paintings to the Tsar of Russia finance a month of convalescence in Teplice.

1836 Wilhelm von Kügelgen, son of Gerhard von Kügelgen, who was murdered in 1820, visits Friedrich on 2 March and finds him very ill.

1837 A lengthy article on Friedrich appears in the fourth volume of K. G. Nagler's "Künstler-Lexicon" (Dictionary of Artists).

1840 Friedrich dies on 7 May. He is buried on 10 May in the Trinitatis cemetery in Dresden.

1893 The first critical appraisal to do justice to Friedrich's art appears in the Norwegian language and is found in Andreas Aubert's monograph on Clausen Dahl, in which Friedrich is discussed in several places.

1906 An exhibition in Berlin, featuring paintings and sculptures from the period 1775 to 1875, presents 32 works by Friedrich. This marks the start of the painter's rediscovery, by no means complete even today.

Photo Credits

The publishers wish to thank the museums, private collections, archives and photographers who granted permission to reproduce works and gave support in the making of the book. In addition to the collections and museums named in the picture captions, we wish to credit the following:

AKG Berlin: cover, 27, 30, 40, 41, 50, 53, 55, 62, 72, 74, 94; AKG Berlin / Erich Lessing: 13, 34; Billedgalleri Bergen, photograph Geir S. Johannessen: 69; Bildarchiv Preussischer Kulturbesitz, Berlin: 7, 12 top, 15 top and bottom, 17, 19, 20, 39, 44, 58, 63 bottom, 71, 76/77, 79, 92, 93, 94 left, photograph Elke Walford: 21; © Staatliche Museen zu Berlin – Preussischer Kulturbesitz,
Department of Prints and Drawings, photograph Reinhard Saczewski: 29, photograph Jörg P. Anders: 1, 47; © Staatliche Museen zu Berlin – Preussischer Kulturbesitz, Nationalgalerie, photograph Jörg P. Anders: 6, 14, 32/33, 35, 37 top, 48, 57, 73, 75, 83, 84, 85 top, 89; © Rheinisches Bildarchiv, Cologne: 70 top; Statens Museum for Kunst, Copenhagen, photograph Hans Petersen: 31; Thorvaldsens Museum, Copenhagen, photograph Hans Petersen: 18; © Staatliche Kunstsammlungen Dresden, Gemäldegalerie Neue Meister, photograph Jürgen Karpinski: 16; Museum Folkwang, Essen, photograph J. Nober: 36, photograph Fotoabteilung der Essener Museen: 51; © Staatliche Museen Kassel, photograph
Hensmanns, 1995: 87 top and bottom; Museum der bildenden Künste, Leipzig, photograph Gerstenberger, 1999: 11 bottom, 82, 90/91; Städtische Kunsthalle, Mannheim, photograph Margita Wickenhäuser: 45, 63 top, 95; Musée du Louvre, Paris, photograph RMN: 12 bottom, photograph RMN – Hervé Lewandowski: 54; Österreichische Galerie Belvedere, Vienna, photograph Fotostudio Otto: 8 top, 24/25, 68; Joachim Blauel – Artothek, Weilheim: 60, 85 bottom; Blauel/Gnamm – Artothek, Weilheim: 23; © Kunstsammlungen zu Weimar, Foto-Atelier Louis Held: 22 bottom, photograph Renno: 59